SO THIS IS KOSHER

SO THIS IS KOSHER

A NEW APPROACH TO JEWISH COOKERY

ANN KAYE · HETTY RANCE

WARD LOCK LIMITED · LONDON

© Ann Kaye and Hetty Rance 1986

First published in Great Britain in 1986 by
Ward Lock Limited, 8 Clifford Street
London W1X 1RB, an Egmont Company

House editor Susan Dixon
Designed by Melissa Orrom
Text filmset by MS Filmsetting Limited,
Frome, Somerset

Printed and bound in Italy by New
Interlitho

British Library Cataloguing in Publication Data
Kaye, Ann and Hetty Rance
    So, this is Kosher!: a new approach to
    Jewish cookery.
    1. Cookery, Jewish
    I. Title
    641.5′676   TX724

    ISBN 0-7063-6374-4

Contents

Notes

It is important to follow the metric or imperial measures when using the recipes in this book. Do not use a combination of measures.

All recipes serve four people, unless otherwise specified.

All spoon measures are level.

Acknowledgments

Food photography Paul Webster
Home economist Lorna Rhodes
Stylist Penny Legg

The authors and publisher would like to thank Rabbi I. Broder for his very kind assistance in checking the Kashrut.

Introduction

So, this is kosher! – but what is kosher cookery? Is it the myth that tells us that kosher cookery is stereotyped and stodgy? Is it made up of a limited number of traditional dishes? Are Jewish dietary laws inevitably restrictive? Are many famous international dishes really taboo to the kosher homemaker because they either include milk and meat in the same dish or incorporate non-kosher ingredients?

We don't think so, and we have set out to show that, in a world of changing cookery trends, kosher cookery can be evolved to help the up-to-date cook, be they man or woman, single or married, with or without a family.

We have been able to do this, partly because of the wide availability of ingredients such as soya milk and parve gelatine and partly because we have used ingredients in a novel way. For example, we have replaced yoghurt with a mixture of soya milk and lemon juice, and have made creamy thick sauces with egg yolks rather than using any dairy products.

We do not want people to abandon their traditional cuisine but we do want to expand kosher culinary horizons into adventurous new ground, and to reflect the changing patterns in Jewish family life which tend today to be centred less around the home than they were in the past. These too are now increasingly influenced by the popularity and ease of foreign travel, the availability of foreign foods and restaurants plus a wealth of books and magazines featuring delicious looking yet 'out of bound' recipes.

Our message is that many such fashionable recipes can be prepared so that they conform to all the requirements of the Jewish dietary laws, yet lose none of their authentic flavour and appearance. Whether Coquilles St Jacques, traditionally made with shellfish, Beef Stroganoff which combines soured cream and milk or Chinese recipes such as Chop Suey and Spare Ribs, both based on pork, all can be adapted to suit the most Orthodox of homes.

When we tried these recipes on family and friends, they looked bewildered. Additionally, the first time we served Cream of Chicken Soup and ended a meat meal with a creamy rice pudding, the look of disbelief on their faces had to be seen to be believed. Once they had tried the recipes, they soon, however, appreciated what we were doing, and their eating habits have never looked back.

Our Passover section continues this theme, and includes

quiches, flans, éclairs and even lasagne – how different from the monotony of matzos and macaroons!

Once you have used the recipes in this book, you will find that there are many others that need not be disregarded on the grounds of kashrut (koshering), and that our ideas can be easily adapted without compromising any of the basic laws.

So, if you are a traditional kosher cook wishing to break new ground, or even if you simply wish to reflect the current trend towards lighter eating, then this is the book for you.
Enjoy!

Ann Kaye and Hetty Rance

Guide To Jewish Dietary Laws

The word 'kosher' means that the selection and preparation of foods has been carried out in accordance with traditional Jewish ritual and dietary laws.

These state that only four-legged animals such as sheep, goats, deer and cattle that chew the cud and have cloven hooves can be eaten. To be kosher, however, these animals must be ritually slaughtered by an official trained in the laws of kashrut, and then checked rigorously for any sign of illness or disease. Only the forequarters of these permitted animals can be eaten.

All birds apart from birds of prey and scavengers, are permitted. Once they have been ritually slaughtered and examined, the neck veins, claws and skin of the feet must be removed.

Following this, the meat must be kashered by soaking it in cold water for 30 minutes in a container kept only for that purpose. It is then rinsed and sprinkled with salt on all surfaces, then put on a special kashering board which is tilted to allow the blood to run away. After 1 hour, it should be rinsed very thoroughly and is then ready for use – it can be frozen at this stage. Any eggs found in poultry should be kashered and used only with meat meals.

Some butchers and poulterers will kasher meat for you, and most frozen meat is already kashered but it is very important to check that this has been done before it is cooked.

Liver is, however, kashered in a different way. It should be cut open with a knife kept especially for the purpose, then rinsed in cold water and sprinkled with salt all over. Grill or sear it until cooked on all sides, then rinse well.

Meat and milk (dairy milk) must be kept apart at all times, which means that separate dishes, utensils and washing-up bowls are kept for meat and milk meals.

Milk and recipes containing milk or other dairy products may be eaten before meat at a meal, although the mouth should be 'cleaned' by eating bread for example, in between. There should be an interval of at least 3 hours before eating milk or dairy products after meat.

Fish must have removable scales and fins – no shellfish is allowed, but fish does not have to be kashered. Fish is parve; this means that it may be eaten immediately before or after meat if it is not prepared with any dairy product, but it must not be cooked together with the meat or eaten from the same dish.

Cheese should be marked as kosher.

Eggs may be used in either milk or meat dishes but if there is any blood in the yolk, the whole egg must be discarded. Eggs of non-kosher birds are not allowed.

Fruit and vegetables should be examined closely to make sure they are not wormy – small fruit like raspberries should be thrown away if they are, while larger fruit such as apples, should have any bad parts cut away.

Flour, pasta, rice, etc should be carefully inspected for mites before use.

When buying jellies, ice cream and confectionery, ensure that they are labelled with the stamp of a Rabbinical authority. They should not contain any animal fats or non-kosher setting agent. Similarly with any packaged product, especially cakes, biscuits and canned foods, and, in particular baby foods.

Passover

During the eight days of the Passover festival, certain other foods are not allowed. You are not permitted to use dried beans and peas, legumes and grains, flour, ordinary baking powder, baking soda and yeast – although a special Passover baking powder is available. Wheat flour is replaced by matzo meal in varying degrees of fineness, and by potato flour. Other foods must have been supervised during packaging, and marked *Kosher lePesach* by a Rabbinical authority. To ensure that no forbidden food comes into contact with permissible Passover foods, it is necessary to change all crockery, cutlery, cooking utensils and washing-up bowls. Some kitchen utensils made of metal or glass may, however, be koshered for Passover by various methods – a local rabbi will advise on the best way to do this.

Any food or drink made by fermenting wheat, rye, barley or oats is also not permitted; this excludes bread, cereals, beer and whisky.

This is a summary of the basic dietary laws; if you are in any doubt or wish to have further information, a rabbi should be consulted.

Principal Ingredients

Soya milk is a vegetable product made from soya beans, and is low in cholesterol. The milk is made by soaking the beans, grinding them, straining and boiling them gently, then straining off and using the resulting liquid.

Soya milk can be found in health food shops and supermarkets and is available in different forms. The most usual is a long life pack but you should also be able to find concentrated (double strength) *soya milk* which we use in some of our recipes. This is suited to recipes which need a thicker, creamier sauce.

Soya milk is also available in powdered form and is useful as a stand-by, although we found it was not suitable for our ice cream recipes. Follow the instructions on the packet when reconstituting it.

Tofu is soya milk curdled with vegetable extract, then drained and pressed to varying degrees of firmness. It is suitable for sweet and savoury dishes – we have used it to make a satisfying soup. It is also available from health food shops.

Soy sauce is made by the natural fermentation of soya beans, wheat, salt and sugar, and is useful as a flavouring – particularly for Chinese recipes, to give an authentic, oriental taste.

Both soya milk and its by-products are cheap, nutritious, high in protein and low in fat, and can be used with both meat and milk recipes. They are not, however, suitable for Passover as soya beans are not permissible for Ashkenazi (European) Jews at this time.

Kosher vegetarian block margarine is a very acceptable substitute for butter and suet, while *soft vegetarian margarine* is particularly suited to recipes such as mock creams, which need a softer texture.

Parve gelatine from Israel is best for recipes which require setting, but it can be difficult to obtain. If so, use vegetable gel powder which is available from health food shops.

Wine vinegar is most useful for recipes which need a subtler flavour than that provided by ordinary vinegar. If a kosher version cannot be obtained, substitute a combination of red or white wine and vinegar in equal proportions.

Firsts

Don't look for traditional chopped liver and chicken soup – they aren't here! What you will find in this chapter are recipes for Mock Lobster Mayonnaise – a colourful dish, and rather cheaper than the original. Also more economical to make than its antecedent is Mock Coquilles St Jacques, served hot and an unusual beginning to your meal.

It is said by people who eat snails that the main flavour comes from the garlic butter; Champignons à L'Escargot omits the snails and the butter, and uses vegetarian margarine and garlic to make an aromatic, quick and easy start to any meal. We continue to travel the world – to Mexico with Enchillada Molé, using the South American combination of chocolate, nuts and a spicy tomato sauce combined with shredded meat, and wrapped in tortillas – a sophisticated taste. Our Pâté Maison isn't all it seems – it's meatless, using a spicy lentil mixture, and can be served from a terrine or in individual portions.

We have not forgotten soups, of course, and if you cannot part from a soup with chicken, you have a choice between Cream of Chicken Soup or Chinese Chicken and Sweetcorn Soup – combine this latter with Spring Rolls (page 44) and two or three other Chinese recipes in the book, and you have a Chinese feast. There can be few cheaper soups to make than Cream of Onion – and if you thought soups were just for the cold weather, try Georgian Cucumber Soup – and think again!

Aubergine Caviar

2 large aubergines
oil for greasing
1 clove of garlic, finely
    chopped
1 × 15ml spoon/1 tablespoon
    grated onion
2 × 15ml spoons/2 tablespoons
    olive oil
lemon juice
salt, freshly ground black
    pepper

GARNISH
lemon twists **or** spirals

Put the aubergines in a greased ovenproof dish, and bake in a moderate oven, 180°C/350°F/Gas 4, for about 40 minutes until soft. Leave to cool, then cut in half and scoop out the flesh. Pass it through a food mill, then mix thoroughly with the garlic and onion, and add the oil. Alternatively, process the vegetables in a blender or food processor with the oil. Add lemon juice to taste, and season well. Serve well chilled, garnished with lemon twists or spirals, and accompanied by hot toast.

Chestnut Balls

Serve as part of a cocktail canapé selection.

275g/10 oz canned, unsweetened chestnut purée
1 medium onion, finely chopped
3 × 15ml spoons/3 tablespoons fine matzo meal
1 × 15ml spoon/1 tablespoon freshly chopped parsley
1 × 5ml spoon/1 teaspoon ground cumin
1 × 5ml spoon/1 teaspoon dried sage
2 eggs, beaten
salt, freshly ground black pepper
matzo meal for coating
oil for shallow frying

Mix together the chestnut purée, onion, matzo meal, parsley, cumin, sage and beaten eggs, then season to taste.

With damp hands, form the mixture into small, walnut-sized balls, adding a little extra matzo meal if required. Roll each ball in matzo meal, and shake off the surplus. Shallow fry gently in hot oil until golden-brown, then drain well, and serve warm.

Potato Balls

450g/1 lb cooked potatoes, mashed
100g/4 oz cooked peas
1 × 15ml spoon/1 tablespoon freshly chopped mint
2 × 15ml spoons/2 tablespoons lemon juice
2 × 15ml spoons/2 tablespoons fine matzo meal
salt, freshly ground black pepper
matzo meal for coating
oil for shallow frying

Beat together the potatoes, peas, mint, lemon juice, matzo meal and seasoning to form a fairly smooth paste.

With damp hands, form the mixture into smooth, walnut-sized balls, adding a little extra matzo meal, if required. Roll each ball in matzo meal, and shake off the surplus. Shallow fry in hot oil until golden-brown, then drain well, and serve hot.

Pâté Maison

Although tasting like meat, this pâté is meat-free and can be served at any meal.

350g/12 oz red lentils
a pinch of ground allspice
1 × 5ml spoon/1 teaspoon
  ground cumin
1 clove garlic, crushed
1 vegetarian stock cube
175g/6 oz vegetarian block
  margarine
350g/12 oz onions, roughly
  chopped
2 × 5ml spoons/2 teaspoons
  sugar
salt, freshly ground black
  pepper
1 × 5ml spoon/1 teaspoon
  parve gelatine
100ml/4 fl oz water
a few drops liquid caramel **or**
  brown colouring
1 × 5ml spoon/1 teaspoon soy
  sauce

GARNISH
bay leaves, juniper berries,
  mace, gherkin fans, olives,
  dried rose-hips **or** citrus
  peel

Put the lentils in a large saucepan, and add the allspice, cumin, garlic and stock cube. Barely cover with cold water, and bring to the boil, stirring all the time. Simmer until very thick and smooth, stirring all the time. Add more water to prevent sticking, if required.

Melt the margarine in a large frying pan, and cook the onion and sugar until the onion browns and caramelizes, stirring all the time. Add to the lentils, and season to taste.

Pour the mixture immediately into individual ramekins or one 15cm/6 inch soufflé dish, and leave to cool.

Meanwhile, dissolve the gelatine in a pan with the water, caramel and soy sauce. Heat until the liquid is clear; do not let it reach boiling point.

Spoon a little of this 'aspic' over the cooled pâté, and garnish as liked. Top with a little more 'aspic', and leave to set.

Serve with Melba toast and curls of vegetarian block margarine.

Note This pâté has a freezer storage life of 2 months. Do not garnish.

Champignons à L'Escargot

Mushrooms in garlic 'butter' are cheap to make and quite delicious – serve with bread to mop up the juices. Flat mushrooms are best for this recipe but if they are not available, use button mushrooms, and keep the stalks for another dish.

2–3 cloves garlic, crushed
2 × 15ml spoons/2 tablespoons
  finely chopped parsley
50g/2 oz vegetarian block
  margarine, softened
450g/1 lb mushrooms

Work the garlic and parsley into the margarine, and spread a little into the cup of each mushroom.

Line a grill pan with foil, and grill the mushrooms over fairly high heat until the garlic 'butter' has melted. Serve at once.

Pâté Maison

Eggs Mimosa

4 cold hard-boiled eggs
1 recipe quantity vegetarian
  white sauce (page 87)
salt, freshly ground white
  pepper
4 slices hot toast

GARNISH
chopped parsley
tomato wedges

Separate the whites from the yolks, and chop. Grate the yolks or press them through a fine sieve.

Mix the chopped whites with the white sauce, then season to taste and heat gently, stirring all the time. Pour the sauce over the hot toast, and pile the sieved egg yolk on top. Garnish with chopped parsley and tomato wedges.

Oeufs Provençales

4 eggs

SAUCE
2 × 15ml spoons/2 tablespoons
  cooking oil
1 medium onion, finely
  chopped
1 clove of garlic, chopped
1 small green pepper, de-
  seeded and finely chopped
1 small red pepper, de-seeded
  and finely chopped
1 × 15ml spoon/1 tablespoon
  flour
400g/14 oz canned tomatoes,
  roughly chopped, juice
  reserved
225ml/8 fl oz water
1 × 15ml spoon/1 tablespoon
  concentrated tomato purée
1 × 2.5ml spoon/½ teaspoon
  dried oregano
1 × 2.5ml spoon/½ teaspoon
  dried basil
1 × 15ml spoon/1 tablespoon
  vinegar
2 × 5ml spoons/2 teaspoons
  soy sauce
salt, freshly ground black
  pepper

Make the sauce first. Heat the oil in a large frying pan, and cook the onion until transparent, stirring all the time. Add the garlic, and cook for a further minute. Add the chopped peppers, and toss together well, continuing to cook until the peppers have softened. Sprinkle with the flour, and stir well to spread it evenly and absorb any juices. Add the remaining sauce-ingredients, and season to taste. Cover the pan, then leave to cook for 15–20 minutes until the vegetables are soft and the liquid is reduced by about half.

Spoon the sauce into four large ramekins, and keep hot in a moderate oven, 180°C/350°F/Gas 4.

Break the eggs into individual bowls, keeping the yolks whole.

Remove the ramekins from the oven one by one, swirl each egg round in its bowl, then pour carefully into the centre of each ramekin. Return to the oven, and bake for 6–8 minutes until the whites of the eggs appear set. Carefully spoon some sauce from the edges of the dish over each egg, and serve immediately, piping hot.

Note The sauce can be made in advance, but must be used very hot.

Baked Eggs and Mushrooms

25g/1 oz vegetarian block margarine
100g/4 oz mushrooms, thinly sliced
2 eggs
225ml/8 fl oz soya milk
salt, freshly ground black pepper

Melt the margarine in a medium-sized frying pan, and fry the mushrooms until they begin to soften, stirring occasionally.

Beat together the eggs and soya milk, and season well.

Divide the cooked mushrooms between four small ramekins, and pour over the egg and soya milk mixture. Stand them in a baking tin containing 2.5cm/1 inch hot water. Bake in a moderate oven, 180°C/350°F/Gas 4, for 35–40 minutes until the custard is set. Serve hot, as a light supper dish, with hot crusty bread.

Mock Coquilles St Jacques

Smoked and fresh cod fillets replace the more usual non-kosher scallops.

450g/1 lb potatoes, peeled
1 egg yolk
75g/3 oz butter
225g/8 oz smoked cod fillet
225g/8 oz fresh cod fillet
150ml/¼ pint white wine
1 small onion, chopped
50g/2 oz button mushrooms, sliced
25g/1 oz flour
50ml/2 fl oz single cream
salt, freshly ground black pepper
juice of ½ lemon
a pinch of grated nutmeg
grated cheese

Boil the potatoes until tender, then mash with the egg yolk and 25g/1 oz butter, making sure there are no lumps.

Poach the smoked fish for 5 minutes in water, then drain and flake it. Poach the fresh fish in the white wine, adding a little water if needed to cover it, then drain and flake it, reserving the cooking liquid. Make it up to 300ml/½ pint with water, if required.

Melt the remaining butter in a pan, and cook the onion until soft and transparent. Add the mushrooms, and stir well. Sprinkle in the flour, then cook for a further 1–2 minutes. Add the smoked and fresh fish, the reserved cooking liquid and the cream, and simmer for 10 minutes, stirring all the time. Season to taste, then stir in the lemon juice and nutmeg.

Pipe a ring of mashed potatoes around the rims of four china scallop-shaped dishes or heatproof saucers, and divide the fish equally between the dishes, piling it carefully into the centre of each. Sprinkle each portion with a little grated cheese, then brown under a hot grill, and serve at once.

Mock Lobster Mayonnaise

A colourful starter suitable for a dinner party.

225g/8 oz thick cod fillet
300ml/½ pint well flavoured
    vegetable stock
2 × 15ml spoons/2 tablespoons
    paprika
lettuce leaves
4 × 15ml spoons/4 tablespoons
    mayonnaise
4 anchovy fillets

GARNISH
capers

Poach the fish in the vegetable stock for 5 minutes, then drain. Separate into large flakes, then leave to cool. Dry the flakes on absorbent paper, then toss them gently in the paprika to colour them – it is not necessary to achieve an even colour, and, in fact, looks better if some pieces are redder than others.

Finely shred the lettuce leaves, and place in individual sundae glasses or salad bowls. Arrange the fish neatly on top, and top with the mayonnaise. Cut the anchovy fillets into half lengthways and then again widthways, then arrange them in a trellis design on top of the mayonnaise. Garnish with the capers.

Tuna Roulade

SERVES 6

3 eggs, separated
25g/1 oz brown sugar
a pinch of salt
100g/4 oz ground almonds
oil for greasing

FILLING
200g/7 oz canned tuna fish in
    brine, drained
300ml/½ pint mayonnaise
1 × 15ml spoon/1 tablespoon
    freshly chopped parsley
6–8 cocktail gherkins,
    chopped
salt, freshly ground black
    pepper

GARNISH
shredded lettuce

Put the egg yolks in a bowl, and whisk them well, then add the sugar and salt, and continue to whisk briskly for 7 minutes.

Whisk the egg whites in a separate bowl until stiff, then fold them gently into the egg yolk mixture. Fold in the ground almonds.

Line a 30 × 20cm/12 × 8 inch Swiss roll tin with greased greaseproof paper, and spread the mixture evenly. Bake in a moderate oven, 180°C/350°F/Gas 4, for 12–15 minutes until firm and light brown. Turn out very carefully on to another sheet of greaseproof paper set on a damp tea-towel, and leave until cold.

Meanwhile, prepare the filling by mixing together all the ingredients, and seasoning to taste.

When the roulade is cold, remove the lining paper, spread the filling evenly over the 'cake', then roll up. Serve cut into slices on a bed of shredded lettuce.

Tuna Roulade

Enchillada Molé

The use of chocolate in the sauce gives an authentic Mexican flavour, and one that is very smooth and creamy.

175g/6 oz cooked chicken, beef **or** turkey, shredded
8 tortillas (page 92)
½ onion, finely chopped

SAUCE
2 × 15ml spoons/2 tablespoons cooking oil
2 small chillies, de-seeded with the veins removed (see **Note**)
1 × 15ml spoon/1 tablespoon sesame seeds
1 × 15ml spoon/1 tablespoon blanched peanuts
1 × 15ml spoon/1 tablespoon blanched almonds
1 × 5ml spoon/1 teaspoon ground cinnamon
1 × 15ml spoon/1 tablespoon soft brown sugar
1 slice of stale bread, crusts removed
a large pinch of salt
300ml/½ pint hot water
50g/2 oz plain parve chocolate

Make the sauce first. Heat the oil in a small pan, and cook the chillies, sesame seeds, peanuts and almonds until brown, tossing frequently. Cool slightly, then pound together in a pestle and mortar. Add the cinnamon, sugar, bread, salt and hot water, and mix well. Alternatively, process the mixture in a blender or food processor.

Return the mixture to the pan, and bring to the boil. Add the chocolate, then simmer until thick, stirring all the time.

Put a little meat on each tortilla, add a little chopped onion, then roll up into sausage shapes.

To serve, spoon some of the sauce over each tortilla, and sprinkle with the remaining onion. Serve hot.

Note Use rubber gloves when handling the chillies.

Cream of Green Pea Soup

40g/1½ oz vegetarian block margarine
40g/1½ oz plain flour
1 beef stock cube
1 litre/1¾ pints hot water
150ml/¼ pint soya milk
450g/1 lb fresh peas, shelled and cooked **or** 275g/10 oz frozen peas, cooked
8–10 pea pods **or** a sprig of fresh mint
salt

GARNISH
mint leaves

Melt the margarine in a medium-sized saucepan, and cook the flour for 2–3 minutes, stirring all the time; do not let the mixture brown. Crumble in the stock cube, then add the water and soya milk, stirring all the time while bringing it to the boil.

Pass the peas through a sieve or purée in a blender or food processor. Add to the pan, together with the pea pods or mint, and add salt to taste. Bring the soup back to the boil, then simmer for 10 minutes, stirring all the time. Season to taste, then remove the pea pods or mint. Garnish with mint leaves, and serve with Garlic Croûtons (page 92).

Cream of Brussels Soup

This soup is equally delicious when served well chilled.

25g/1 oz vegetarian block margarine
1 small potato, peeled and finely sliced
1 small onion, finely sliced
1 clove of garlic, crushed
225g/8 oz Brussels sprouts
1 beef stock cube
600ml/1 pint boiling water
150ml/¼ pint soya milk
bouquet garni
a large pinch of grated nutmeg
salt, freshly ground black pepper
1 egg yolk

Melt the margarine in a medium-sized saucepan, and toss the potato, onion and garlic gently in the fat for about 10 minutes until the onion is transparent but not brown. Stir in the Brussels sprouts, and toss them for about 3 minutes well coated and hot. Crumble in the stock cube, then add the boiling water, soya milk, bouquet garni and nutmeg, and season to taste. Bring to the boil, then reduce the heat, cover, and simmer for 20 minutes until the vegetables are soft. Pass through a sieve or purée in a blender or food processor.

Beat the egg yolk with a little cold water, then stir gently into the soup. Re-heat carefully without boiling.

Serve with Garlic Croûtons (page 92).

Cream of Onion Soup

75g/3 oz vegetarian block margarine
450g/1 lb Spanish onions, finely sliced
50g/2 oz plain flour
450ml/¾ pint hot water
450ml/¾ pint soya milk
salt, freshly ground black pepper

Melt the margarine in a large saucepan, and toss the onions well to coat them thoroughly. Cover the pan, then cook the onions very gently on low heat for 10–15 minutes until very soft and transparent. Stir occasionally to prevent the onions burning. Sprinkle with the flour, and mix together well. Cook for 2–3 minutes so that the flour cooks but does not burn. Stir in the water and soya milk, and bring to the boil, stirring carefully. Season to taste with salt and pepper, and stir again, then cover and simmer for 10–15 minutes.

Pass half the soup through a sieve or purée in a blender or food processor. Return to the pan, and stir well. Re-heat carefully without boiling.

Serve with Mandelen (page 93).

Tomato and Tofu Soup

1 × 15ml spoon/1 tablespoon
  cooking oil
1 medium onion, finely
  chopped
2 medium tomatoes, skinned
  and chopped
275g/10 oz silken tofu
450ml/¾ pint soya milk
a pinch of oregano
salt, freshly ground black
  pepper
2 × 15ml spoons/2 tablespoons
  concentrated tomato purée

GARNISH
chopped parsley

Heat the oil in a saucepan, and cook the onion for 2–3 minutes until transparent, stirring all the time. Add the tomatoes, and continue cooking for a further 2–3 minutes.

Using either a blender or food mill, purée the tomato and onion mixture with the tofu, then combine it with the milk, oregano and seasoning. Return to the pan, bring to the boil, then simmer for 10 minutes.

Mix the tomato purée with a little cold water, then add to the soup, and simmer for 2–3 minutes. Garnish with the chopped parsley.

Cream of Chicken Soup

600ml/1 pint soya milk
1 bay leaf
1 small onion, sliced
1 × 2.5ml spoon/½ teaspoon
  ground nutmeg
a blade of mace
a sprig of thyme **or** parsley
6–8 black peppercorns
50g/2 oz vegetarian block
  margarine
50g/2 oz plain flour
600ml/1 pint chicken stock
100g/4 oz cooked **or** uncooked
  chicken, finely shredded
salt, freshly ground black
  pepper

GARNISH
chopped parsley

Put the soya milk, bay leaf, onion, nutmeg, mace, thyme or parsley and the peppercorns in a small saucepan, and bring slowly to the boil. Remove from the heat, cover tightly, and put to one side for 15 minutes.

Meanwhile, melt the margarine in a medium-sized saucepan, and cook the flour for 2–3 minutes, stirring all the time; do not let the mixture brown. Gradually blend in the stock, stirring well to prevent lumps forming. Bring to the boil, add the shredded chicken and season with salt and pepper.

Strain the milk mixture, then add it to the soup. Stir well and simmer gently for 10–15 minutes, then season to taste and thin down with extra stock if it is too thick. Garnish with chopped parsley, and serve with Mandelen (page 93) or Garlic Croûtons (page 92).

Chicken soups with a difference
FROM THE TOP Cream of Chicken Soup, Chinese Chicken and Sweetcorn Soup (page 24) **and** Georgian Cucumber Soup (page 24) **accompanied by** Aunt Celia's Mandelen (page 93)

Chinese Chicken and Sweetcorn Soup

3 × 5ml spoons/3 teaspoons
 cornflour
a small piece of ginger root,
 peeled and finely chopped
100g/4 oz uncooked chicken,
 chopped
2 × 5ml spoons/2 teaspoons
 sherry
600ml/1 pint chicken stock
salt, freshly ground black
 pepper
100g/4 oz canned sweetcorn
 kernels, drained
1 egg white, lightly beaten

GARNISH
spring onions, finely chopped

Follow this with Beef Chop Suey (page 29) to continue the Chinese theme.

Mix the cornflour with a little water to make a smooth paste.
 Mix together the ginger root, chicken and sherry.
 Put the stock into a large saucepan, and bring it to the boil. Add the chicken mixture, salt, pepper and sweetcorn, and simmer for 5 minutes, stirring well. Add the cornflour mixture, stirring all the time, and cook for 1 minute. Just before serving, add the egg white, still stirring. Garnish with spring onions, and serve at once.

Georgian Cucumber Soup

1 cucumber, peeled and finely
 chopped
3 pickled gherkins, finely
 chopped
175g/6 oz cooked chicken,
 diced
4 spring onions (including the
 green tops), chopped
2 hard-boiled eggs, chopped
2 × 5ml spoons/2 teaspoons
 French mustard
1 × 5ml spoon/1 teaspoon
 caster sugar
salt, white pepper
300ml/½ pint concentrated
 soya milk
600ml/1 pint chicken stock
 (see **Note**)
150ml/¼ pint white wine
3–4 sprigs mint
fresh dill **or** 1 × 5ml spoon/1
 teaspoon dried dill

GARNISH
mint leaves

An easy to prepare, 'no-cook' summer soup.

Mix together the cucumber, gherkins, chicken, spring onions and eggs.
 Mix together the mustard, sugar, salt and pepper, then mix gradually with the soya milk, stock and wine. Add the mint and dill, then mix in the chopped vegetables. Chill for at least 1–2 hours before serving so that the flavours can blend. Remove the mint and fresh dill, if used, before serving, and garnish with mint leaves.

Note It is particularly important to skim the chicken stock thoroughly to eliminate any fat globules.

Feeding the Family

This is the chapter that will appeal equally to the feeder of hungry mouths and to the man or woman, home from work who wants to eat well, yet both quickly and economically. It is often not the cooking that presents the problems but deciding what to cook. It is all too easy to fall into the routine of cooking the same dozen or so meals time after time. Some solutions are offered here, comprising a host of ideas to make you think again about what it is possible to make.

Most people have cooked sausages – but had you ever thought it was possible to make them into Toad in the Hole? If you don't like meat sausages at all, try our cheesy ones – larger sizes for a main meal, smaller ones for a party, and served with a milk meal. You will find the recipe for Scotch Eggs in the Passover chapter – and of course, there's no reason why you can't make them the rest of the year. If, however, you want to cut down on meat, why not try our Vegetarian Scotch Eggs, covered with chopped nuts and potatoes. In fact, the covering is so tasty, you can make it and serve as patties.

We continue out international flavour here as well – there's Pastitsio from Greece, Bobotie from South Africa and recipes from Mexico and China, all of which will give your cooking a worldwide perspective.

Mexican Mix

Mexicans get up at sunrise and enjoy a substantial mid morning meal similar to this spicy recipe.

50g/2 oz vegetarian block
   margarine
225g/8 oz long-grain rice,
   cooked
1 red pepper, de-seeded and
   chopped
1 small onion, chopped
200g/7 oz canned sweetcorn
   kernels, drained
1 × 15ml spoon/1 tablespoon
   freshly chopped parsley
50g/2 oz stoned olives
100g/4 oz salami, cubed
4 eggs, beaten
$\frac{1}{2}$ × 2.5 ml spoon/$\frac{1}{4}$ teaspoon
   chilli powder
salt, freshly ground black
   pepper

Spread half the margarine thickly on the base of a 25cm × 17.5cm/ 10 × 7 inch shallow gratin dish, and spread the rice evenly over the base and sides.

Mix together the pepper, onion, sweetcorn, parsley, olives, salami and eggs, and season to taste with the chilli powder, salt and pepper. Spoon the mixture evenly into the rice-lined dish, and dot with the remaining margarine. Cook in a moderate oven, 180°C/350°F/Gas 4, for 25–30 minutes until the mixture is heated through.

Serve with a green salad topped with thinly sliced Spanish onion.

Quiche Bologna

250g/9 oz prepared shortcrust
   pastry (page 89)
flour for rolling out
2 slices Bologna **or** other
   salami-type meat, cut into
   small segments
150ml/$\frac{1}{4}$ pint soya milk
salt, freshly ground black
   pepper
2 eggs, lightly beaten
3 spring onions, chopped
grated nutmeg

Roll out the pastry on a lightly floured surface to fit a 20cm/8 inch flan tin. Prick the base with a fork, and bake blind in a fairly hot oven, 200°C/400°F/Gas 6, for 20 minutes. Leave until cool.

Carefully arrange half the salami segments in the case. Beat together the soya milk, seasoning and eggs, and pour the mixture into the flan case. Carefully lay the remaining segments on top to form a circle. Arrange the chopped spring onions in the centre. Grate a little nutmeg over the top, and bake in a fairly hot oven, 190°C/375°F/Gas 5, for 25–30 minutes until the custard has set and risen slightly.

Serve with a green salad.

Using salami
Mexican Mix **and** Quiche Bologna

Toad in the Hole

Ideal for children – and popular with adults, too!

1 × 15ml spoon/1 tablespoon
cooking oil
450g/1 lb frying sausages
1 recipe quantity vegetarian
pancake batter (page 90)

Put the oil in a shallow, ovenproof dish or baking tin, and heat in a hot oven, 220°C/425°F/Gas 7, until the oil is hot. Put the sausages into the tin, and cook for 10 minutes. Remove from the oven, then pour the batter over the sausages, ensuring that the sausages are separated across the dish. Return to the oven, and cook for a further 30 minutes. Reduce the heat to fairly hot, 200°C/400°F/Gas 6, and cook for a further 15 minutes until the batter has set and risen around the sausages. Serve at once.

Crispy Potato and Sausage Pudding

450g/1 lb small potatoes
225g/8 oz spicy sausages
25g/1 oz vegetarian block
margarine
4 hard-boiled eggs, sliced
2 eggs, beaten
300ml/½ pint soya milk
salt, freshly ground black
pepper
a pinch of grated nutmeg

Boil the potatoes in their skins, then peel and slice them while still hot.

Grill the sausages gently until brown and cooked through, then slice them.

Coat a 25cm/10 inch gratin dish with about one-quarter of the margarine. Put the sliced potatoes, sausages and hard-boiled eggs into the dish, and mix together, arranging a row of the sliced potatoes around the edge.

Mix the beaten eggs with the soya milk, and season with the salt, pepper and nutmeg. Pour this over the potato, sausage and egg mixture, and dot with the remaining margarine. Bake in a fairly hot oven, 200°C/400°F/Gas 6, for 25–30 minutes until the top is crisp and brown.

Serve with broccoli.

Beans Portugaise

Using salami and egg yolks instead of ham and cream, this is a substantial and economical meal.

25g/1 oz vegetarian block margarine
1 medium onion, finely chopped
50g/2 oz salami, diced
2 cloves garlic, crushed
450g/1 lb bread beans, fresh or frozen (shelled weight)
75ml/3 fl oz beef stock
1 × 2.5ml spoon/½ teaspoon mixed dried herbs
salt, freshly ground black pepper
2 egg yolks
2 × 5ml spoons/2 teaspoons wine vinegar

GARNISH
chopped parsley

Melt the margarine in a large frying pan, and cook the onion, salami and garlic without browning for 5 minutes until the onion is transparent. Add the beans, stock and dried herbs. Bring to the boil, then cover and simmer for 15–20 minutes until the beans are tender. Season to taste.

Mix together the egg yolks and wine vinegar, and gradually stir into the beans. Heat very gently without allowing the mixture to boil. Serve hot, garnished with chopped parsley.

Variation
For a milk meal, substitute 50g/2 oz smoked salmon for the salami and use vegetable stock instead of beef stock.

Beef Chop Suey

2 × 15ml spoons/2 tablespoons soy sauce
1 × 15ml spoon/1 tablespoon sherry
2 × 5ml spoons/2 teaspoons cornflour
225g/8 oz beef, cut into small stamp size pieces, 0.5cm/¼ inch thick (approx)
5 × 15ml spoons/5 tablespoons cooking oil
2 spring onions, cut into 2.5cm/1 inch lengths
1 small piece of ginger root, finely chopped
2 small carrots, chopped
2 tomatoes, chopped
50g/2 oz mange-tout peas, cut in half widthways
1 small green pepper, de-seeded and chopped
a few cauliflower florets, cut up into fairly small pieces
2 × 5ml spoons/2 teaspoons salt
1 × 15ml spoon/1 tablespoon sugar

Mix together the soy sauce, sherry and cornflour, and use to coat the beef thoroughly.

Heat half the oil in a wok or heavy frying pan, and cook the meat over fairly high heat for about 2 minutes, stirring all the time, until browned all over. Remove from the pan, and keep warm.

Heat the rest of the oil in the pan, and stir-fry the spring onions and ginger for 30 seconds before adding the remaining vegetables, and, finally, the salt and sugar. Stir-fry for about 1 minute, then add the cooked meat. Cook for a further 2 minutes, adding a little water, if necessary, to prevent any drying out. Serve at once, with plain boiled rice.

Variation
This recipe can also be made with chicken or turkey and the vegetables varied according to season.

Beef and Vegetable Flan

1 recipe quantity prepared
    shortcrust pastry (page 89)
flour for rolling
25g/1 oz vegetarian block
    margarine
225g/8 oz onions, chopped
225g/8 oz carrots, chopped
100g/4 oz mushrooms,
    chopped
100g/4 oz pressed beef, diced
2 eggs
1 × 2.5ml spoon/½ teaspoon
    mustard powder
150ml/¼ pint soya milk
salt, freshly ground black
    pepper

Roll out the pastry on a lightly floured surface to fit a 22.5cm/
9 inch flan tin. Prick the base with a fork, and bake blind in a fairly
hot oven, 200°C/400°F/Gas 6, for 20 minutes. Leave until cool.

Meanwhile, melt the margarine in a large frying pan, and toss the
onions and carrots in the pan for a few minutes until they start to
soften. Add the mushrooms and meat, and continue to stir-fry until
the meat is heated through. Transfer the mixture to the hot flan
case.

Beat the eggs with the mustard powder, soya milk and seasoning,
and pour the mixture into the flan case. Bake in a moderate oven,
180°C/350°F/Gas 4, for about 25–30 minutes until the filling has set
and risen slightly. Serve hot, with jacket potatoes, or cold, with a
salad.

Note If preparing the recipe in advance to serve hot, make sure that
the flan case and filling are cold before assembling, and chill the
uncooked flan until ready to bake.

Variations
1. Use 450g/1 lb onions cut into rings; omit the carrots and
mushrooms.
2. Use 100g/4 oz onions chopped and lightly stir-fried, and
substitute 100g/4 oz canned asparagus spears and 100g/4 oz cooked
chopped chicken for the carrots, mushrooms and beef. Omit the
mustard powder.

INDIVIDUAL BEEF AND VEGETABLE FLANS
Line four 10cm/4 inch foil flan cases with the pastry but do not
bake blind. Add the filling, and bake in a fairly hot oven,
190–200°C/375–400°F/Gas 5–6, until the pastry begins to brown.
Reduce the heat to moderate, 180°C/350°F/Gas 4, and continue to
cook until the filling has set.

Picadillo

By using minced beef and oil in place of the non-kosher meats and fats normally associated with Mexican cookery, we can re-create this very popular dish.

2 × 15ml spoons/2 tablespoons
  cooking oil
1 medium onion, chopped
1 clove of garlic, chopped
1 green pepper, chopped
3 green chillies, de-seeded and
  finely chopped
450g/1 lb minced beef
400g/14 oz canned tomatoes,
  chopped, juice reserved
3 small parboiled potatoes,
  cut into 1.25cm/½ inch
  cubes
40g/1½ oz stoned olives
25g/1 oz flaked almonds
25g/1 oz raisins
25g/1 oz candied peel,
  chopped
1 banana, sliced
5cm/2 inch stick cinnamon
2 cloves
2 bay leaves
a sprig of fresh thyme
1 × 15ml spoon/1 tablespoon
  freshly chopped parsley
2 × 5ml spoons/2 teaspoons
  brown sugar
salt, freshly ground black
  pepper

Heat the oil in a medium-sized pan, and cook the onion until golden, stirring all the time. Add the garlic, pepper and chillies, and continue cooking until the pepper is soft and beginning to colour. Stir in the meat and break up well. Continue cooking until the meat is brown. Add the tomatoes and their juice, and simmer until the mixture is thick, stirring all the time. Add the potatoes, olives, almonds, raisins, candied peel and banana slices.

Tie together the cinnamon, cloves, bay leaves and thyme with white cotton, and tie to the side of the pan. Add the parsley, sugar and seasoning. Cover tightly and simmer for 25–30 minutes, stirring occasionally, until the meat is thoroughly cooked and the mixture starts to dry. Discard the tied spices.

Serve on a bed of rice, accompanied by Tortillas (page 92).

Lasagne

175g/6 oz dried lasagne (see
  Note)
5 × 15ml spoons/5 tablespoons
  cooking oil
1 × 5ml spoon/1 teaspoon salt
1 medium onion, chopped
1 clove of garlic, chopped
100g/4 oz carrots, chopped
50g/2 oz button mushrooms,
  thinly sliced
350g/12 oz minced beef
50g/2 oz concentrated tomato
  purée
450ml/¾ pint water
2 × 15ml spoons/2 tablespoons
  finely chopped parsley
1 × 5ml spoon/1 teaspoon
  dried basil
2 × 5ml spoons/2 teaspoons
  dried oregano
1 × 5ml spoon/1 teaspoon
  sugar
1 beef stock cube
50g/2 oz dried breadcrumbs

SAUCE
600ml/1 pint soya milk
1 small onion, sliced
a sprig of fresh thyme **or** a
  pinch of dried thyme
a pinch of grated nutmeg
1 bay leaf
50g/2 oz vegetarian block
  margarine
50g/2 oz plain flour
salt, freshly ground black
  pepper
1 × 5ml spoon/1 teaspoon
  mustard powder

Cook the lasagne in a large pan of steadily boiling water until *al dente* with 1 × 15ml spoon/1 tablespoon of the oil and the salt. Drain thoroughly.

Heat the remaining oil in a saucepan. Stir in the chopped onion, garlic and carrots, and cook together gently until soft and transparent. Add the mushrooms and minced beef, and continue cooking until the meat is well browned, stirring all the time. Stir in the tomato purée, water, parsley, basil, oregano and sugar, and crumble in the stock cube. Bring to the boil, stirring all the time, then reduce the heat, cover and simmer for 25 minutes, stirring occasionally.

To make the sauce, heat the soya milk gently in a separate pan with the sliced onion, thyme, nutmeg and bay leaf until it is just boiling. Remove the pan from the heat, cover tightly and leave to infuse for about 15 minutes.

Melt the margarine in a saucepan, and cook the flour for 3 minutes, stirring all the time. Strain the infused soya milk through a fine sieve, and gradually blend into the mixture. Bring to the boil, stirring all the time, then simmer for 2–3 minutes until the sauce begins to thicken. Season to taste, then add the mustard powder.

Spread a thin layer of the meat mixture over the base of a 20 × 25 cm/8 × 10 inch greased ovenproof dish, then add a thin layer of the sauce. Cover with a layer of lasagne. Continue with these layers until all the ingredients are used up, finishing with a layer of sauce. Sprinkle with the breadcrumbs, and cook in a fairly hot oven, 200°C/400°F/Gas 6, for 25–30 minutes until the top is crisp and bubbly.

Serve with a crisp green salad.

Note There are acceptable lasagnes which do not need pre-cooking. If using them, halve the quantity of flour and margarine for the white sauce; this will make a thinner sauce.

Pastitsio

This recipe, found in many Greek tavernas, traditionally uses cheese and cream. Our version uses a non dairy white sauce.

450g/1 lb macaroni
4 × 15ml spoons/4 tablespoons cooking oil
salt, freshly ground black pepper
1 large onion, chopped
2 cloves garlic, finely chopped
450g/1 lb minced beef
150ml/¼ pint red wine
225g/8 oz tomatoes, skinned and chopped
½ × 2.5 ml spoon/¼ teaspoon ground nutmeg
3 × 15ml spoons/3 tablespoons concentrated tomato purée
1 × 5ml spoon/1 teaspoon dried oregano
50g/2 oz fresh wholemeal breadcrumbs
450ml/¾ pint vegetarian white sauce (page 87)

Cook the macaroni in a large pan of steadily boiling water until *al dente* with 1 × 15ml spoon/1 tablespoon of the oil and 1 × 5ml spoon/1 teaspoon salt.

Meanwhile, heat the remaining oil in a large frying pan, and cook the onion and garlic until transparent, stirring all the time. Add the meat, and continue cooking, stirring, until well browned. Drain off any excess fat, if necessary. Add the wine, tomatoes, nutmeg, salt, pepper, tomato purée and oregano, and stir well, then reduce the heat, and cook for 15 minutes, stirring occasionally.

Drain the macaroni thoroughly, and put half into a large greased casserole. Sprinkle with half the breadcrumbs, and pour the meat sauce over. Cover with the remaining macaroni, and coat carefully with the white sauce, making sure that all the macaroni is covered. Sprinkle with the remaining breadcrumbs. Bake in a fairly hot oven, 200°C/400°F/Gas 6, for 35–40 minutes until the dish is heated through and bubbling. Serve cut into squares, accompanied by a green salad.

Chilli Con Carne

Adjust the amount of chilli powder to make the recipe more or less spicy, according to your taste-buds!

1 × 15ml spoon/1 tablespoon cooking oil
1 medium onion, chopped
2 cloves garlic, chopped
1 green pepper, de-seeded and chopped
450g/1 lb minced beef
2 × 5ml spoons/2 teaspoons chilli powder
400g/14 oz canned tomatoes, roughly chopped
425g/15 oz canned **or** dried red kidney beans (see **Note**)
salt, freshly ground black pepper

Heat the oil in a frying pan, and cook the onion and garlic until transparent, stirring all the time, then cook the pepper and minced beef until browned. Add the chilli powder, and continue to cook, stirring well, to ensure that the chilli powder cooks. Add the tomatoes and kidney beans, and stir well. Season well to taste. Reduce the heat, cover and cook for 1 hour, stirring occasionally.

Serve with rice and a green salad.

Note If using dried kidney beans, soak them overnight in cold water, then discard the water. Cover with fresh water, and cook in a large pan of unsalted, boiling water, making sure that they boil rapidly for at least 10 minutes. Add salt to the water when the beans are almost cooked. The length of the cooking time will vary according to the freshness of the beans but should be between 45 minutes–1 hour.

Chinese Beef Noodles

2 × 15ml spoons/2 tablespoons
  cooking oil
1 clove of garlic, finely
  chopped
450g/1 lb minced beef
1 small green pepper, de-
  seeded and cut into thick,
  matchstick lengths
2 carrots, cut into thick,
  matchstick lengths
4 spring onions, cut into
  matchstick lengths
450g/1 lb cooked noodles
1 × 15ml spoon/1 tablespoon
  sherry
1 × 15ml spoon/1 tablespoon
  soy sauce
1 × 5ml spoon/1 teaspoon
  honey
1 × 5ml spoon/1 teaspoon
  vinegar
1 × 5ml spoon/1 teaspoon
  concentrated tomato purée
1 × 2.5ml spoon/½ teaspoon
  salt

Heat the oil in a large frying pan or wok, and stir-fry the garlic over high heat for 30 seconds, stirring well until it begins to brown. Add the minced beef, and cook until it is well browned, stirring all the time. Reduce the heat slightly, then add the pepper, carrots and spring onions, and stir-fry for about 1 minute. Add the remaining ingredients, and heat through, stirring all the time. Serve at once, accompanied by jasmin tea.

Bobotie

Our version of a spicy South African dish usually made with a milk sauce.

2 × 15ml spoons/2 tablespoons
  cooking oil
1 medium onion, chopped
1 clove of garlic, chopped
2 × 5ml spoons/2 teaspoons
  curry powder
450g/1 lb minced beef
1 × 15ml spoon/1 tablespoon
  chopped nuts
salt, freshly ground black
  pepper
150ml/¼ pint soya milk
1 egg, beaten

Heat the oil in a frying pan, and cook the onion and garlic until transparent, stirring all the time. Add the curry powder, and cook for 2 minutes, stirring well. Add the meat, and brown thoroughly before mixing in the chopped nuts. Season to taste. Transfer the mixture to an ovenproof casserole.

Mix together the soya milk and egg, and pour the mixture over the meat. Cook in a moderate oven, 180°C/350°F/Gas 4, for 45 minutes until the custard is set.

Serve with rice and mango chutney.

Chinese Beef Noodles

Barbecued Spare Ribs

Breast of lamb with the surplus fat removed and cut into strips makes a good substitute for the more usual pork in this well known recipe.

1 × 15ml spoon/1 tablespoon
 paprika
1 × 2.5ml spoon/½ teaspoon
 ground coriander
salt, freshly ground black
 pepper
675g/1½ lb lamb spare ribs, fat
 removed, and cut into
 2.5cm/1 inch strips

BARBECUE SAUCE
1 small onion, finely grated
1 clove of garlic, crushed
1.25cm/½ inch slice ginger
 root, finely grated
1 × 15ml spoon/1 tablespoon
 soft brown sugar
1 × 15ml spoon/1 tablespoon
 honey
2 × 15ml spoons/2 tablespoons
 soy sauce
2 × 15ml spoons/2 tablespoons
 vinegar
1 × 15ml spoon/1 tablespoon
 tomato ketchup
1 × 5ml spoon/1 teaspoon
 mustard powder
1 × 5ml spoon/1 teaspoon
 paprika
1 × 5ml spoon/1 teaspoon
 chilli sauce
½ × 2.5ml spoon/¼ teaspoon
 five-spice powder
2 × 15ml spoons/2 tablespoons
 orange juice
salt, freshly ground black
 pepper

Mix together the paprika, coriander and seasoning, and rub into the lamb strips. Grill them under high heat for 10–15 minutes until browned all over, turning frequently, then put them in a single layer in a roasting tin.

Mix together the ingredients for the sauce, and pour this over the spare ribs. Bake in a moderate oven, 180°C/350°F/Gas 4, for 30–35 minutes, basting occasionally, until the sauce is reduced and the meat is crisp and brown.

Serve with plain boiled rice.

Lamb and Apple Pie

This recipe uses leftover lamb to make an unusual supper dish.

450g/1 lb cooked lamb, minced
oil for greasing
1 large onion, sliced
1 large cooking apple, peeled and sliced
1 × 2.5ml spoon/½ teaspoon dried rosemary, crumbled
1 × 2.5ml spoon/½ teaspoon dried sage, crumbled
salt, freshly ground black pepper
300ml/½ pint beef stock
1 × 15ml spoon/1 tablespoon concentrated tomato purée
350g/12 oz prepared shortcrust pastry (page 89)
flour for rolling out
beaten egg

Put a thin layer of meat in a greased 1.2 litre/2 pint ovenproof dish, then add one layer each of the sliced onion and apple. Continue layering until the meat, onion and apple have been used up. Sprinkle with the rosemary, sage, salt and pepper. Mix together the stock and tomato purée, and pour this over the meat.

Roll out the pastry on a lightly floured surface, and use to cover the dish. Decorate with pastry trimmings, and make a hole in the centre to allow the steam to escape while cooking. Brush with the beaten egg, and bake in a very hot oven, 230°C/450°F/Gas 8, for 10 minutes. Reduce the heat to moderate, 180°C/350°F/Gas 4, and cook for a further 25–30 minutes until the pastry is browned and the filling well cooked.

Lamb Cutlets en Croûte

A simple and cheap supper dish.

450g/1 lb minced lamb
1 medium onion, finely chopped
1 × 2.5ml spoon/½ teaspoon dried rosemary, crumbled
1 egg, beaten
2 × 15ml spoons/2 tablespoons flour
salt, freshly ground black pepper
1 × 15ml spoon/1 tablespoon cooking oil
350g/12 oz prepared puff pastry (page 90)
mint jelly
beaten egg for glazing

Mix together the lamb, onion, rosemary, egg, flour and seasoning. Divide the mixture into eight portions, then shape them into fairly stubby lamb chop shapes.

Heat the oil in a medium-sized frying pan, and fry the 'chops' carefully for a few minutes on each side until lightly browned. Drain on absorbent paper.

Roll out the pastry on a lightly floured surface fairly thinly, and divide into eight pieces. Brush each piece, lightly with mint jelly, place a 'chop' on each piece, and brush the edges with beaten egg. Seal each parcel, and brush the outsides with the remaining egg. Decorate with any pastry trimmings, and place on a baking tray with the pastry seam underneath. Bake in a hot oven, 220°C/425°F/Gas 7, for 25–30 minutes until the pastry is risen and lightly browned.

Tomato-baked Lamb

A simple dish to make; once it is in the oven, just forget about it until ready to serve.

2 × 15ml spoons/2 tablespoons
    cooking oil
1 medium onion, sliced
1 clove of garlic, chopped
4 lamb chops
400g/14 oz canned tomatoes,
    roughly chopped, juice
    reserved
1 × 5ml spoon/1 teaspoon
    dried rosemary, crumbled
225g/8 oz long-grain rice
1 bay leaf
salt, freshly ground black
    pepper
300ml/½ pint water

Heat the oil in a frying pan, and cook the onion and garlic until transparent, stirring all the time. Add the chops, and cook them on both sides until browned. Add the tomatoes and their juice, the rosemary, rice and bay leaf, then season well. Pour into a medium sized ovenproof dish, add the water, stir, then cover and cook in a moderate oven, 180°C/350°F/Gas 4, for 1 hour until the rice is cooked and the water has been absorbed. Discard the bay leaf.

Serve with a green vegetable and mint sauce.

Southern Chicken with Corn Fritters

An easy way to give a 'Deep South' feel to your cookery.

4 chicken portions
flour for coating
2 eggs, beaten
medium matzo meal for
    coating
75g/3 oz vegetarian block
    margarine
3 × 15ml spoons/3 tablespoons
    cooking oil
150ml/¼ pint soya milk
100g/4 oz plain flour, sifted
salt, freshly ground black
    pepper
225g/8 oz canned sweetcorn
    kernels, drained

GARNISH
2 bananas, cut into quarters
4 slices canned pineapple,
    drained and halved

Coat the chicken portions with the flour, then dip first in the beaten eggs and then in the matzo meal, pressing it in firmly. Chill for at least 10 minutes to allow the coating to set.

Heat half the margarine and half the oil in a large frying pan, and fry the chicken pieces until brown all over. Remove from the pan with a perforated spoon, and put in an ovenproof dish. Cover and cook in a fairly hot oven, 200°C/400°F/Gas 6, for 35–40 minutes until cooked through.

Meanwhile, add the remaining beaten egg to the soya milk, and mix well. Gradually stir in the flour to make a batter, then season to taste, and stir in the sweetcorn kernels.

Heat the remaining margarine and oil in the frying pan, then drop in tablespoons of batter, and fry quickly until brown on each side. Remove with a perforated spoon, and keep hot.

Dust the banana quarters with flour, then fry in the remaining fat until browned. Drain well, then fry the pineapple slices until brown. Drain well.

Serve the chicken with the corn fritters and fruit.

Southern Chicken with Corn Fritters

Chicken and Walnut Flan

SERVES 3–4

225g/8 oz prepared shortcrust pastry (page 89)
flour for rolling out
300ml/½ pint vegetarian white sauce (page 87)
175–225g/6–8 oz cooked chicken, chopped
25g/1 oz walnuts, roughly chopped
salt, freshly ground black pepper
1 × 2.5ml spoon/½ teaspoon paprika

Roll out the pastry on a lightly floured surface to fit a 17.5 cm/7 inch flan tin. Prick the base with a fork, and bake blind in a fairly hot oven, 200°C/400°F/Gas 6, for 20 minutes. Leave until cool.

Meanwhile, mix together the white sauce, chicken and walnuts, and season to taste.

Put the mixture into the flan case, and sprinkle the paprika on top. Bake in a moderate oven, 180°C/350°F/Gas 4, for 20–25 minutes until the filling has set and risen slightly.

Serve with a green salad as a light supper dish.

Chicken in Lemon Sauce

SERVES 4–5

1.25–1.5kg/2½–3 lb chicken, skinned and cut into serving portions
1 bay leaf
bouquet garni
2 lemons, sliced and de-pipped
salt, freshly ground black pepper
50g/2 oz vegetarian block margarine
50g/2 oz plain flour
300ml/½ pint soya milk

GARNISH
chopped parsley
orange and lemon slices

Put the chicken portions in a single layer in a shallow saucepan. Barely cover with water, bring to the boil, skim, then add the bay leaf, bouquet garni, lemon slices and seasoning. Cover the pan and simmer for about 1 hour or until tender. Remove the chicken portions with a perforated spoon, put on a warmed serving dish, and keep hot.

Strain the stock remaining in the pan, then return to the pan and boil vigorously, uncovered, until reduced to about 300ml/½ pint liquid.

Melt the margarine in a small pan, and cook the flour for 2–3 minutes, stirring all the time; do not let the mixture brown. Slowly blend in the reduced stock and the soya milk, and bring to the boil, still stirring, until it thickens. Remove the pan from the heat, and season to taste.

Coat the chicken with the sauce, and garnish with the chopped parsley, orange and lemon slices.

Chicken and Tomato Bake

An unusual way to turn a little cooked chicken into a substantial meal, using eggs and stock to make a creamy sauce.

100g/4 oz vegetarian block margarine
40g/1½ oz plain flour
300ml/½ pint chicken stock
150ml/¼ pint white wine
1 × 2.5ml spoon/½ teaspoon ground nutmeg
salt, white pepper
2 egg yolks
275g/10 oz cooked chicken, chopped
1 × 15ml spoon/1 tablespoon cooking oil
1 medium onion, sliced
2 cloves garlic, crushed
400–450g/14–16 oz canned tomatoes, chopped
1 × 15ml spoon/1 tablespoon concentrated tomato purée
1 × 5ml spoon/1 teaspoon dried basil
1 × 5ml spoon/1 teaspoon dried oregano
4 slices brown bread, 2cm/¾ inch thick, crusts removed, and cut into cubes
40g/1½ oz dried breadcrumbs

Melt 40g/1½ oz of the margarine in a small saucepan, and cook the flour for 1–2 minutes, stirring all the time; do not let the mixture brown. Stir in the stock, wine and nutmeg, and season to taste. Bring to the boil, stirring all the time until the sauce thickens. Remove the pan from the heat, beat in 15g/½ oz margarine, a little at a time, then beat in the egg yolks until the sauce is white and creamy. Re-heat the sauce gently until it thickens, stirring carefully, then add the chopped chicken, and pour the mixture into a large casserole.

Heat the oil in a small saucepan, and cook the onion and garlic gently until soft and golden, stirring all the time. Add the tomatoes, tomato purée, basil, oregano and salt and pepper. Cook for 6–8 minutes until the mixture is well blended and reduced by about one-third. Spoon the tomato mixture gently over the chicken sauce, and cover with the cubed bread.

Melt the remaining margarine in a pan, and mix with the breadcrumbs. Sprinkle them on top of the casserole, spreading them evenly. Bake in a fairly hot oven, 200°C/400°F/Gas 6, for 20–25 minutes until the top is crisp and brown.

Serve with cauliflower or broccoli.

Turkey in Mustard Sauce

50g/2 oz plain flour
salt, freshly ground black pepper
450g/1 lb turkey meat, breast or thigh, cut into 2cm/¾ inch cubes
50g/2 oz vegetarian block margarine
1 medium onion, finely chopped
2 × 5ml spoons/2 teaspoons prepared English mustard
1 × 5ml spoon/1 teaspoon lemon juice
150ml/¼ pint concentrated soya milk

GARNISH
lemon butterflies

Season the flour with the salt and pepper, and use to coat the meat lightly.

Melt half the margarine in a saucepan, and fry the meat for about 5–7 minutes until cooked through, turning to make sure that all sides are browned. Remove from the pan with a perforated spoon, transfer to a warmed serving dish, and keep hot.

In a separate pan, melt the remaining margarine, and cook the onion for 4–5 minutes until soft, stirring all the time. Stir in the remaining seasoned flour, and cook for 2–3 minutes, without browning. Mix in the mustard, lemon juice and soya milk, and cook for 2–3 minutes until bubbling.

Pour the sauce over the turkey, and garnish with lemon butterflies.

Serve with plain boiled potatoes.

Pasta Bake

175g/6 oz whole brown lentils
0.5cm/¼ inch slice ginger root
175g/6 oz mixed spinach and
    wholewheat pasta twists
1 × 15ml spoon/1 tablespoon
    cooking oil
1 × 5ml spoon/1 teaspoon salt
2 egg yolks
450ml/¾ pint vegetarian white
    sauce (page 87)
fresh breadcrumbs

LENTIL SAUCE
2 × 15ml spoons/2 tablespoons
    cooking oil
1 large onion, chopped
1 clove of garlic, finely
    chopped
400g/14 oz canned tomatoes,
    chopped, juice reserved
2 × 15ml spoons/2 tablespoons
    concentrated tomato purée
1 × 5ml spoon/1 teaspoon
    dried basil
1 × 2.5ml spoon/½ teaspoon
    dried oregano
1 × 5ml spoon/1 teaspoon
    ground cinnamon
½ × 2.5ml spoon/¼ teaspoon
    ground cloves
2 bay leaves
2 × 5ml spoons/2 teaspoons
    brown sugar
salt, freshly ground black
    pepper

Soak the lentils overnight in water. Discard the water, then add the ginger. Barely cover with cold water, and bring to the boil, stirring all the time. Simmer until soft, stirring all the time. Add more water to prevent sticking, if required.

To make the sauce, heat the oil in a pan, and cook the onion and garlic gently until golden, stirring all the time. Add the tomatoes with their juice, the tomato purée, basil, oregano, cinnamon, cloves, bay leaves, sugar and seasoning to taste. Cook gently until thick, add the beef, if using, and heat it in the sauce.

Drain the lentils thoroughly, and add to the sauce.

Cook the pasta in a large saucepan of steadily boiling water until *al dente* with the oil and salt. Drain thoroughly.

Spread the pasta on the base of a 25cm/10 inch square gratin dish, and cover with the lentil sauce.

Mix the egg yolks into the white sauce, and spread on top of the dish. Sprinkle with the breadcrumbs, and bake in a moderate oven, 180°C/350°F/Gas 4, for 45–50 minutes until browned and well heated through.

Serve with a salad.

Variation
To make a meat meal, use only 100g/4 oz lentils and add 75–100g/3–4 oz cold roast beef to the thickened sauce before adding the lentils.

Creamed Eggs

25g/1 oz vegetarian block
    margarine
25g/1 oz plain flour
salt, freshly ground black
    pepper
300ml/½ pint soya milk
4 hard-boiled eggs, sliced
1 × 15ml spoon/1 tablespoon
    freshly chopped parsley
cooked rice **or** mashed
    potatoes
a pinch of paprika

Melt the margarine in a small saucepan. Season the flour with salt and pepper, then stir it into the hot fat, and cook for 1–2 minutes without browning; stir all the time. Gradually stir in the soya milk, and stir until the sauce thickens. Add the sliced eggs and the parsley, season to taste, then heat through gently.

Serve on a bed of rice or hot mashed potatoes, and sprinkle with paprika.

Serve with salami and grilled tomatoes.

Vegetarian Scotch Eggs

2 × 15ml spoons/2 tablespoons
  cooking oil
1 medium onion, finely
  chopped
1 × 15ml spoon/1 tablespoon
  flour
150ml/¼ pint water
1 × 15ml spoon/1 tablespoon
  concentrated tomato purée
2 × 5ml spoons/2 teaspoons
  dried mixed herbs
225g/8 oz nuts, finely chopped
  and ground (see **Note**)
50g/2 oz medium matzo meal
175g/6 oz cold mashed
  potatoes
1–2 eggs, beaten
salt, freshly ground black
  pepper
4 hard-boiled eggs
matzo meal for coating
oil for deep frying

Heat the oil in a frying pan, and cook the onion until soft and golden, stirring all the time. Stir in the flour, and cook for 3–4 minutes, allowing it to brown slightly. Add the water gradually, then cook until the mixture becomes a thick paste. Mix in the tomato purée and herbs, and remove the pan from the heat. Add the nuts, matzo meal, mashed potato and enough of the beaten egg to make a firm paste. Season to taste.

With damp hands, work the mixture round the eggs in an even layer. Roll the covered eggs in the remaining beaten egg, then toss gently in the matzo meal, pressing it in firmly. Chill for at least 15 minutes before frying so that the mixture firms up.

Heat the oil to 160°C/325°F, and deep fry the eggs, two at a time, until golden-brown all over. This should take about 5–6 minutes. Drain on absorbent paper.

Note Use either all peanuts or a mixture of nuts.

Variation
Any leftover mixture can be shaped into patties, 1.25–2cm/½–¾ inch thick, and fried until brown.

Cheesy Sausages

These look and taste like ordinary meat sausages but can be served with milk meals. They can also be made cocktail size and are excellent combined with fruit and cheese cubes.

100g/4 oz fresh white
  breadcrumbs
2 × 15ml spoons/2 tablespoons
  freshly chopped chives
2 × 15ml spoons/2 tablespoons
  freshly chopped parsley
1 × 5ml spoon/1 teaspoon
  freshly chopped thyme
1 × 5ml spoon/1 teaspoon
  mustard powder
150g/5 oz hard cheese, grated
salt, freshly ground black
  pepper
2 eggs
dried breadcrumbs for coating
oil for shallow frying

Mix the breadcrumbs with the herbs, mustard powder, cheese, salt and pepper. Add one whole egg and the yolk of the second; reserve the second egg white.

Divide the mixture into 8–10 large or about 20 smaller portions, then roll into sausage shapes.

Beat the second egg white slightly.

Dip each sausage shape first into the beaten egg white, then roll in the dried breadcrumbs. Shallow fry gently in hot oil until brown all over, then drain well.

Serve with baked jacket potatoes.

Spring Rolls

3 × 15ml spoons/3 tablespoons
   vegetable oil
1 medium onion, thinly sliced
1 clove of garlic, chopped
1.25cm/½ inch slice ginger
   root, shredded
2 stalks celery, thinly sliced
1 medium carrot, coarsely
   grated
100g/4 oz cabbage **or** Chinese
   leaves, thinly sliced
100g/4 oz bean sprouts,
   cleaned (see **Note**)
50g/2 oz mushrooms, thinly
   sliced
salt, freshly ground black
   pepper
1 recipe quantity vegetarian
   pancakes (page 90)
beaten egg
oil for deep frying

Heat the oil in a large frying pan, and stir-fry the onion, garlic and ginger for 2 minutes to soften slightly. Add the celery, carrot, cabbage, bean sprouts and mushrooms, and continue to stir-fry for a further 5 minutes so that the vegetables are cooked but still crisp. Season to taste, then leave to cool.

Place a tablespoon of the filling at one end of a pancake on the browned side. Fold over the sides, then brush gently with the beaten egg. Fold over the top to enclose the filling, then roll up. Seal the end well with beaten egg, and put the seal underneath. Repeat until both the pancakes and filling have been used up.

Heat the oil to 180°C/350°F, and deep fry the pancakes for 3–4 minutes until crisp and golden. Drain on absorbent paper, and serve hot, with Sweet and Sour Sauce.

Variation
A small quantity of cooked, shredded chicken or turkey can be added to the filling for a meat meal.

Sweet and Sour Sauce

1 × 15ml spoon/1 tablespoon
   vegetable oil
1 small onion, very finely
   chopped
1 clove of garlic, finely
   chopped
1.25cm/½ inch slice ginger
   root, grated
1 × 15ml spoon/1 tablespoon
   concentrated tomato purée
25ml/1 fl oz vinegar
25g/1 oz sugar
1 × 2.5ml spoon/½ teaspoon
   salt
1 × 2.5ml spoon/½ teaspoon
   paprika
75ml/3 fl oz pineapple juice
225ml/8 fl oz water
2 × 5ml spoons/2 teaspoons
   potato flour

Heat the oil in a small saucepan, and cook the onion, garlic and ginger until soft but not brown, stirring all the time. Add the tomato purée, vinegar, sugar, salt, paprika, pineapple juice and half the water, then bring to the boil and cook gently for 10 minutes.

Mix the potato flour with the remaining water, then add to the pan and use to thicken the sauce. Bring back to the boil, stirring all the time. Taste and add a little more vinegar, if necessary.

Feeling Flush

We all like to push the boat out from time to time, and here we offer ideas for the cook who wants to impress, with recipes that may need a little more time or money spent on them, but which will produce dishes that will repay that extra investment. Spaghetti Carbonara, for example, makes a little smoked salmon go a long way and could be served as a speedy starter or a quick and impressive supper dish. Chicken and Mushroom Pancakes may take a little longer to prepare but most of it can be done in advance. Oriental Grilled Chicken and Pineapple uses leftovers to make an exotic meal. Veal Suprême uses humble stewing veal to produce a classic creamy dish while Beef Satay is simple, yet served with its accompanying sauce, produces an exotic flavour not usually found in kosher cookery.

You will also find such classics as Beef Wellington and Beef Stroganoff, and there are also colourful dishes – how about Layered Meat Gâteau – easy to make, with all preparations carried out beforehand, yet guaranteed to surprise when you bring it to the table.

Spaghetti Carbonara

SERVES 4 as a starter
SERVES 2 as a main meal

Spaghetti Carbonara is traditionally made with bacon but this smoked salmon version is said to be very close to the original.

225g/8 oz spaghetti
4 × 15ml spoons/4 tablespoons olive oil
salt, freshly ground black pepper
1 clove of garlic, crushed
50g/2 oz smoked salmon, finely chopped
25g/1 oz butter, chopped
3 × 15ml spoons/3 tablespoons single cream
2 eggs, beaten
a pinch of Cayenne pepper
25g/1 oz Parmesan cheese, grated

Cook the spaghetti in a large pan of steadily boiling water until *al dente* with 1 × 15ml spoon/1 tablespoon of the oil and 1 × 5ml spoon/1 teaspoon salt.

Meanwhile, heat the remaining oil in a large frying pan, and cook the garlic until transparent, stirring all the time. Add the chopped salmon, and continue to cook until it turns crisp and slightly brown. Keep warm.

Drain the spaghetti thoroughly, then return to the saucepan. Add the butter, and toss the pasta over low heat until the butter melts and coats it.

Stir the cream into the salmon mixture, and heat until it bubbles. Remove from the heat, then add the eggs, salt, pepper and Cayenne pepper, and mix together well.

Pile the pasta on to a hot serving dish, pour the mixture over, toss well, and sprinkle with the Parmesan cheese. Serve at once.

Beef Satay

Impress your friends and family with some Indonesian cookery.

450g/1 lb beef, cubed

MARINADE
a strip of lemon rind
2 medium onions, roughly
    chopped
1 × 15ml spoon/1 tablespoon
    soy sauce
1–2 × 15ml spoons/1–2
    tablespoons cooking oil
2 × 5ml spoons/2 teaspoons
    ground coriander
1 × 5ml spoon/1 teaspoon
    ground cumin
1 × 5ml spoon/1 teaspoon
    ground turmeric
$\frac{1}{2}$ × 2.5ml spoon/$\frac{1}{4}$ teaspoon
    ground cinnamon
50g/2 oz roasted peanuts
1 × 5ml spoon/1 teaspoon salt
1 × 5ml spoon/1 teaspoon
    sugar

Make the marinade first. Grind the lemon rind, onions, soy sauce, 1 × 15ml spoon/1 tablespoon of cooking oil, the coriander, cumin, turmeric and cinnamon in a food mill or process in a blender until well mixed. Add the peanuts, salt and sugar, and continue processing until a thick paste is formed; add the remaining oil, if required, to draw the mixture together.

Pour the marinade on to the meat in a bowl, and coat the meat well in it. Leave for at least 1 hour.

Thread the meat on to skewers, allowing about six cubes of meat per skewer. Grill until well done, basting occasionally with the marinade and turning the skewers.

Serve with rice and Satay Sauce.

Variation
Substitute chicken or turkey for the beef.

Satay Sauce

1 × 15ml spoon/1 tablespoon
    cooking oil
2 medium onions, finely
    chopped
75g/3 oz roasted peanuts
1 × 2.5ml spoon/$\frac{1}{2}$ teaspoon
    chilli powder
150ml/$\frac{1}{4}$ pint warm water
1 × 5ml spoon/1 teaspoon
    brown sugar
salt
1 × 15ml spoon/1 tablespoon
    soy sauce
juice of $\frac{1}{2}$ lime **or** lemon

Heat the oil in a pan, and cook half the onions until transparent, stirring all the time. Pound the remaining onions, the peanuts and chilli powder in a pestle or process in a blender until smooth. Add to the cooked onion, and continue to cook for a few minutes, stirring all the time. Gradually add the warm water and sugar, and mix in thoroughly. Season with the salt, then add the soy sauce and fresh lime or lemon juice. Serve hot.

Beef Satay **and** Satay Sauce

Beef Stroganoff

2 × 15ml spoons/2 tablespoons
   cooking oil
2 medium onions, sliced
100g/4 oz mushrooms, sliced
2 × 15ml spoons/2 tablespoons
   flour
salt, freshly ground black
   pepper
1 × 5ml spoon/1 teaspoon
   mustard powder
450g/1 lb ball of the rib steak,
   cut into strips
   (2.5 × 0.75cm/1 × ¼ inch)
1 × 15ml spoon/1 tablespoon
   brandy
1 × 15ml spoon/1 tablespoon
   concentrated tomato purée
150ml/¼ pint chicken stock
2 × 15ml spoons/2 tablespoons
   lemon juice
150ml/¼ pint soya milk

GARNISH
chopped parsley

Heat half the oil in a pan, and cook the onions until pale golden, then add the mushrooms, and cook for a further 2 minutes. Remove from the heat.

Season the flour with salt, pepper and mustard powder, and use to coat the meat lightly.

Heat the remaining oil in a separate pan, and fry the meat until browned. Add the cooked onion and mushroom mixture, together with any cooking liquid, and simmer for 5 minutes, stirring occasionally.

Pour the brandy over the meat, and ignite it. When the flames have subsided, stir in the tomato purée and chicken stock, and bring to the boil, stirring carefully. Pour in the lemon juice and soya milk, and stir again, then cover and simmer for 15 minutes. Garnish with chopped parsley.

Serve on a bed of rice.

Chinese Fried Beef

1 × 15ml spoon/1 tablespoon
   sherry
1 × 15ml spoon/1 tablespoon
   chilli sauce
1.25cm/½ inch piece ginger
   root, finely chopped
4 spring onions, finely
   chopped
450g/1 lb ball of the rib steak,
   cut into stamp size pieces
oil for deep frying

BATTER
4 × 15ml spoons/4 tablespoons
   flour
a pinch of salt
1 egg
3–4 × 15ml spoons/3–4
   tablespoons water

Prepare the batter first. Sift the flour and salt into a bowl, make a well in the centre, then add the egg and water. Beat well to form a smooth batter, then leave to stand for 30 minutes. Beat well again before using to ensure that no lumps of flour remain.

Put the sherry, chilli sauce, ginger, spring onions and meat into a bowl, mix well, then leave to marinate for 30 minutes. Remove the meat from the marinade with a perforated spoon

Heat the oil to 180°C/350°F, dip the meat into the batter, and deep fry for 3–4 minutes until golden-brown. Drain on absorbent paper. Serve hot, with soy sauce.

Beef Wellington

This classic recipe is traditionally made with fillet of beef from the hindquarters. As this cut is not available to the kosher cook, we have par-cooked the meat before finishing it off with its pastry jacket.

3 × 15ml spoons/3 tablespoons cooking oil
1.5kg/3 lb ball of the rib joint
salt, freshly ground black pepper
1 recipe quantity prepared puff pastry (page 90)
flour for rolling out
beaten egg for glazing

MUSHROOM FILLING
50g/2 oz vegetarian block margarine
1 small onion, finely chopped
100g/4 oz mushrooms, finely chopped
salt, freshly ground black pepper
25g/1 oz plain flour
75ml/3 fl oz white wine
150ml/¼ pint strong beef stock
1 × 15ml spoon/1 tablespoon freshly chopped parsley

Heat the oil in a roasting tray. Season the joint with salt and pepper, and brown it quickly all over in a hot oven, 220°C/425°F/Gas 7, for 10 minutes. Reduce the heat to moderate, 180°C/350°F/Gas 4, and cook for 1 hour (medium roast, 70°C/150°F on a meat thermometer) until the meat is lightly cooked. Remove the meat from the oven, and leave to cool completely.

Meanwhile, prepare the mushroom filling. Melt the margarine in a small pan, and cook the onion until transparent, stirring all the time. Add the mushrooms, season to taste, then cook until almost dry. Stir in the flour, and cook for a further minute. Add the wine and stock, and cook until the mixture is smooth, stirring all the time. Reduce until the mixture begins to feel stiff. Stir in the parsley, then leave to cool.

Roll out the pastry thinly on a lightly floured surface into an oblong large enough to cover the meat completely.

Spread a layer of the mushroom mixture in the centre of the pastry, and put the meat into the middle. Spread the remaining mushroom mixture all over the meat. Dampen the edges of the pastry with the beaten egg, and completely cover the meat with the pastry, making sure that all the edges are sealed together well.

Put the meat on a baking sheet with the seam underneath, and make two small holes to allow steam to escape. Decorate the top with pastry trimmings, and brush with the remaining beaten egg. Leave to rest in the refrigerator for 30 minutes before baking to allow the pastry to relax. Bake in a hot oven, 220°C/425°F/Gas 7, for about 30–40 minutes until the pastry is golden-brown.

Layered Meat Gâteau

A very colourful dish, cut into slices and served like a cake.

½ recipe quantity vegetarian
  pancakes (page 90)

MEAT LAYER
1 × 15ml spoon/1 tablespoon
  cooking oil
1 medium onion, finely
  chopped
1 clove of garlic, finely
  chopped
350g/12 oz minced beef
50g/2 oz mushrooms, thinly
  sliced
1 small green pepper, de-
  seeded and thinly sliced
1 × 5ml spoon/1 teaspoon
  dried mixed herbs
2 tomatoes, skinned and
  chopped
2 × 15ml spoons/2 tablespoons
  concentrated tomato purée
300ml/½ pint beef stock **or** red
  wine
1 bay leaf
salt, freshly·ground black
  pepper

VEGETABLE LAYERS
350g/12 oz frozen chopped
  spinach
25g/1 oz vegetarian block
  margarine
salt, freshly ground black
  pepper
grated nutmeg
350g/12 oz carrots, chopped

TOMATO SAUCE
1 × 15ml spoon/1 tablespoon
  cooking oil
1 medium onion, finely
  chopped
1 clove of garlic, finely
  chopped
400g/14 oz canned tomatoes,
  roughly chopped, juice
  reserved
1 × 5ml spoon/1 teaspoon
  dried mixed herbs
75ml/3 fl oz red wine
  (optional)
salt, freshly ground black
  pepper

Make the meat layer first. Heat the oil in a large frying pan, and cook the onion and garlic until transparent, stirring all the time. Add the meat, and continue to cook until the meat is browned. Add the mushrooms, pepper, herbs and tomatoes, and cook for 2 minutes, stirring all the time, then add the tomato purée, stock or wine, the bay leaf and seasoning to taste. Reduce the heat and simmer for 30 minutes, stirring occasionally, then remove the bay leaf. The mixture should be fairly dry.

To make the vegetable layers, cook the spinach in a pan over low heat with half the margarine, stirring until cooked. Season with salt, pepper and grated nutmeg.

Boil the carrots in lightly salted water until soft, then mash well. Stir in the remaining margarine, and season with salt, pepper and grated nutmeg.

Line a 17.5cm/7 inch soufflé dish with enough foil to enclose the finished 'cake'. Put a pancake in the base, then add the spinach, spreading it evenly. Cover with another pancake, then spread with the meat mixture in an even layer. Cover with another pancake, then cover with the carrots. Cover with another pancake, then wrap the foil over the top to secure the parcel. Bake in a moderate oven, 180°C/350°F/Gas 4, for 35–40 minutes until the 'cake' is thoroughly heated through.

Meanwhile, make the tomato sauce. Heat the oil in a frying pan, and cook the onion and garlic until transparent, stirring all the time. Add the tomatoes, mixed herbs and red wine, if using, season well, then sieve.

Lift the 'cake' out of the dish, and transfer to a serving plate. Unwrap carefully, and trim the foil neatly round the base of the serving plate before slicing the 'cake' into wedges.

Serve with the hot tomato sauce and a green salad.

Note Most of the preparation can be done in advance; the meat and tomato sauces and the pancakes can be frozen and the 'cake' assembled just before cooking.

Layered Meat Gâteau

Crown Roast of Lamb

1 crown roast of lamb (see **Note**)

STUFFING
100g/4 oz vegetarian block margarine
1 medium onion, finely chopped
2 stalks celery, finely chopped
100g/4 oz mushrooms, finely sliced
100g/4 oz prunes, soaked, pitted and chopped
2 × 15ml spoons/2 tablespoons lemon juice
150g/5 oz medium matzo meal
1 egg, lightly beaten
175ml/6 fl oz boiling water
salt, freshly ground black pepper

GARNISH
cutlet frills **or** glazed carrot balls and small glazed onions

Make the stuffing first. Melt the margarine in a large frying pan, and cook the onion until it is transparent, stirring all the time. Add the celery and mushrooms, and cook until all the vegetables are soft. Remove from the heat, then mix with the prunes, lemon juice, matzo meal, egg and boiling water. Season to taste, and use to fill the centre of the crown roast.

Place in a well-greased baking dish, and cover the stuffing with greased foil. Cook in a fairly hot oven, 190°C/375°F/Gas 5, for 15 minutes, then cook in a moderate oven, 180°C/350°F/Gas 4, allowing 30–35 minutes per 450g/1 lb; baste frequently. Remove the foil from the stuffing for the last 30 minutes of the cooking time. Top each cutlet with a cutlet frill or carrot balls and onions, and serve.

Note Most butchers will prepare a crown roast ready for stuffing. If not, buy two best ends of lamb with 6–7 ribs in each. Trim off most of the fat, and cut about 5cm/2 inches of meat from the thin bone ends, then scrape the bone ends clean.

Make small slits between the base of the ribs. This allows the ends to be joined in a circle with the bones on the outside so that they resemble a crown. Join with fine string.

Wrap the bone ends in foil to stop them burning during cooking.

Veal Suprême

75g/3 oz vegetarian block margarine
225g/8 oz onions, roughly chopped
100g/4 oz carrots, sliced
2–3 stalks celery, sliced
1 small green pepper, de-seeded and roughly chopped
50g/2 oz plain flour
salt, freshly ground black pepper
450g/1 lb stewing veal, cubed
600ml/1 pint soya milk
2 bay leaves

Melt the margarine in a medium saucepan, and cook the vegetables for a few minutes until softened, stirring all the time.

Season the flour with the salt and pepper, and use to coat the veal lightly. Add to the vegetables, and fry until the meat is golden-brown. Sprinkle with any remaining seasoned flour, and cook gently for 1–2 minutes, stirring all the time. Blend in the soya milk, add the bay leaves, and bring to the boil, stirring all the time, until the sauce is smooth and thick. Transfer to an ovenproof dish, and cook, covered, in a moderate oven, 180°C/350°F/Gas 4, for $1-1\frac{1}{4}$ hours until the meat is tender, then remove the bay leaves.

Serve with plain boiled rice.

Osso Buco

What can you usually do with shin of veal other than turn it into soup? This traditional Italian recipe totally transforms this ingredient into something both lavish and colourful.

3 × 15ml spoons/3 tablespoons flour
salt, freshly ground black pepper
675–900/1½–2 lb shin of veal, cut into slices 1.25cm/½ inch thick
4 × 15ml spoons/4 tablespoons cooking oil
1 medium onion, finely chopped
225g/8 oz carrots, finely chopped
2 stalks celery, finely chopped
2 cloves garlic, crushed
150ml/¼ pint dry white wine
150ml/¼ pint chicken stock
400g/14 oz canned tomatoes, chopped
1 × 2.5ml spoon/½ teaspoon dried rosemary
sugar

SAFFRON RICE
225g/8 oz long-grain rice
salt
a pinch of powdered saffron

GREMOLATA GARNISH
4 × 15ml spoons/4 tablespoons finely chopped parsley
grated rind of 2 lemons
2–3 cloves garlic, finely chopped

Season the flour with the salt and pepper, and use to coat the veal lightly.

Heat the oil in a pan large enough to take the veal in one layer. Brown quickly on both sides, then remove from the pan.

Brown the onion, carrots, celery and garlic in the remaining oil, then return the meat to the pan, standing the slices upright so that the marrow does not fall out while cooking. Pour the wine, stock and tomatoes over the meat, then stir in the rosemary. Season and add sugar to taste. Cover the pan and simmer for 1½ hours until the meat is tender.

Meanwhile, make the saffron rice. Cook the rice in boiling salted water until *al dente*. Drain thoroughly, then mix in the saffron.

Mix together the parsley, lemon rind and garlic for the garnish.

Serve the Osso Buco on a bed of saffron rice, and sprinkle the gremolata garnish on top.

Tandoori Chicken

Here again, a combination of lemon juice and soya milk replaces the yoghurt which is used in traditional Indian cookery.

2 × 15ml spoons/2 tablespoons lemon juice

1 × 5ml spoon/1 teaspoon paprika

1½ × 5ml spoons/1½ teaspoons salt

1 × 1.5–1.8kg/3½–4 lb roasting chicken, skinned and cut into 6–8 pieces

MARINADE

2 cloves garlic, crushed

1 small piece of ginger root, finely chopped

1 × 2.5ml spoon/½ teaspoon salt

2 × 15ml spoons/2 tablespoons cooking oil

3 × 15ml spoons/3 tablespoons lemon juice

3 × 15ml spoons/3 tablespoons wine vinegar

1 × 15ml spoon/1 tablespoon ground coriander

1 × 15ml spoon/1 tablespoon ground cumin

1 × 2.5ml spoon/½ teaspoon ground allspice

1 × 2.5ml spoon/½ teaspoon ground nutmeg

1 × 2.5ml spoon/½ teaspoon paprika

a few drops red food colouring

150ml/¼ pint soya milk

GARNISH

shredded lettuce

lemon wedges

Spanish onions, finely sliced

Mix together the lemon juice, paprika and salt. Make slashes in the thick part of each chicken piece, rub the mixture into each piece and especially into the cuts. Leave in a cool place for 20–30 minutes.

To make the marinade, mix the garlic, ginger, salt and 1 × 5ml spoon/1 teaspoon of the cooking oil in a pestle and mortar, and pound to a smooth paste. Mix together the remaining marinade ingredients, and add them to the garlic paste.

Pour the marinade over the chicken pieces, cover the dish and chill for at least 8 hours but up to 24 hours, if possible.

Place the chicken pieces in a single layer in an ovenproof dish. Pour over the marinade, and cook in a fairly hot oven, 200°C/400°F/Gas 6, for 50–60 minutes, basting occasionally. Alternatively, grill the chicken pieces for 15–20 minutes on each side, basting frequently until the pieces are cooked through. To check that they are cooked, pierce with a skewer – the chicken is cooked when the juices are clear, not pink. Garnish with lettuce, lemon wedges and onion rings.

Tandoori Chicken

Chicken and Mushroom Pancakes

1 × 1.8–2kg/4–4½ lb roasting
   chicken **or** fowl
1 onion, quartered
1 carrot, quartered
6 peppercorns
bouquet garni
350g/12 oz mushrooms, sliced
juice of 1 lemon
75g/3 oz vegetarian block
   margarine
75g/3 oz plain flour
salt, freshly ground black
   pepper
300ml/½ pint concentrated
   soya milk
1 recipe quantity vegetarian
   pancakes (page 90)

GARNISH
chopped parsley

Put the chicken, onion, carrot, peppercorns and bouquet garni in a large saucepan, and add enough water to cover the chicken. Bring to the boil, skim, then cover the pan and simmer until tender – about 1 hour for a chicken, 1½ hours for a fowl. Leave to cool in the liquid.

Remove the meat from the bones, and cut it into small, bite-sized pieces. Put to one side. Return the bones to the stock, bring the pan back to the boil and simmer for 1½ hours. Strain, then put in a clean plan to reduce to 900ml/1½ pints.

Put the mushrooms in a pan with the lemon juice and a little water. Cover and cook over high heat for 2–3 minutes, then cool and strain them. Add the mushrooms to the cooked chicken; reserve the cooking liquid.

Melt the margarine in a saucepan, and cook the flour for 2 minutes, stirring all the time. Slowly add the reduced chicken stock, mushroom water and the seasoning. Bring to the boil, continuing to stir, then add the soya milk. Reduce the heat and continue to stir until the sauce thickens, then remove from the heat.

Mix approximately half the sauce with the mixed chicken and mushrooms, and put a spoonful of the mixture on to one-half of a pancake. Fold the other half over, and repeat until both pancakes and mixture have been used up. Arrange the filled pancakes in a greased, shallow, ovenproof dish. Pour the remaining sauce over the top, and re-heat in a moderate oven, 180°C/350°F/Gas 4, for 25–30 minutes until heated through. Sprinkle with the chopped parsley before serving.

Serve with a green salad or vegetables.

Note The pancakes, sauce and filling can be prepared in advance and assembled as required – re-heat thoroughly before serving.

Chinese Chicken

2 × 15ml spoons/2 tablespoons
   cooking oil
1 × 1.4kg/3 lb chicken, skinned
   and chopped through the
   bone into 12 or more pieces
1 medium onion, chopped
150ml/¼ pint water
75ml/3 fl oz soy sauce
75ml/3 fl oz medium sherry
25g/1 oz brown sugar
225g/8 oz canned water
   chestnuts, drained
225g/8 oz canned bamboo
   shoots, drained

Heat the oil in a frying pan, and fry the chicken pieces and onion over high heat for 5 minutes, stirring well. Add the water and soy sauce, and stir well.

Transfer the mixture to a 1.2 litre/2 pint ovenproof dish, and cook in a moderate oven, 180°C/350°F/Gas 4, for 35 minutes. Add the sherry and sugar, and cook for a further 25 minutes. Add the chestnuts and bamboo shoots, stir again and cook for a further 30 minutes to allow the flavours to blend.

Serve with plain boiled rice.

Chicken with Walnuts and Grapes

1 × 1.4–1.6kg/3–3½ lb chicken
  cut into 8 portions
salt, freshly ground black
  pepper
75g/3 oz clear honey
2 × 15ml spoons/2 tablespoons
  cooking oil
25g/1 oz vegetarian block
  margarine
100g/4 oz broken walnuts
100g/4 oz seedless grapes

GARNISH
walnut halves
halved seedless grapes

Season the chicken portions with salt and pepper, and brush with some of the honey.

Heat the oil and margarine in a pan, and sauté the chicken portions, skin side down, for about 7–8 minutes until golden. Turn and cook the other side for about 3–4 minutes until the meat is cooked through. Remove from the pan with a perforated spoon, and keep warm.

Add the remaining honey and the walnuts to the pan, and cook for about 4 minutes, then add the grapes, and cook for a further 2 minutes.

Serve on a bed of rice, surrounded by walnuts and grapes.

Oriental Grilled Chicken and Pineapple   *SERVES 2*

This recipe turns humble leftover chicken into an exotic meal.

4–5 × 15ml spoons/4–5
  tablespoons softened
  vegetarian block margarine
a pinch of ground ginger
a pinch of ground turmeric
a pinch of Cayenne pepper
1 clove of garlic, crushed
1 × 5ml spoon/1 teaspoon
  mango chutney
2 portions cold poached
  chicken, skinned
100g/4 oz long-grain rice
300ml/½ pint cold water
1 × 2.5ml spoon/½ teaspoon
  salt
a pinch of powdered saffron
  or turmeric
4 slices canned pineapple
1 × 15ml spoon/1 tablespoon
  Demerara sugar
2 × 15ml spoons/2 tablespoons
  pine nut kernels **or**
  almonds, toasted

GARNISH
toasted pine nut kernels **or**
  flaked almonds
halved seedless grapes

Cream 2–3 × 15ml spoons/2–3 tablespoons of the margarine with the ginger, turmeric, Cayenne pepper, garlic and chutney until well blended. Spread generously on the outside surfaces of the chicken, and chill for at least 1 hour.

Meanwhile, put the rice, water, salt and saffron into a saucepan, bring to the boil, stir once, cover, then simmer for 12–15 minutes until the liquid has been absorbed and the rice is tender and has separate grains.

Arrange the chicken portions in a shallow, ovenproof dish, and grill until hot and golden-brown.

Melt the remaining margarine in a frying pan, and sauté the pineapple slices until brown on both sides. Sprinkle with the Demerara sugar, and grill quickly until the sugar caramelizes.

Toss the rice with the pine nut kernels or almonds, and spoon on to a flat serving dish. Top with the grilled chicken and pineapple, and pour over any pan juices. Garnish with the toasted nuts and the grapes.

Turkey Steaks in Saffron Sauce

flour for coating
salt, freshly ground black
   pepper
oil for shallow frying
4 turkey breast steaks,
   1.25cm/½ inch thick
   (approx)

SAFFRON SAUCE
40g/1½ oz vegetarian block
   margarine
3 × 15ml spoons/3 tablespoons
   cooking oil
1 large onion, roughly
   chopped
2 cloves garlic, crushed
4–5 tomatoes, skinned, de-
   seeded and chopped
1 bay leaf
5–6 sage leaves **or** 1 × 2.5ml
   spoon/½ teaspoon dried
   sage
a sprig of tarragon **or**
   1 × 2.5ml spoon/½ teaspoon
   dried tarragon
a large pinch of powdered
   saffron
225ml/8 fl oz chicken stock
225ml/8 fl oz dry white wine
1 × 15ml spoon/1 tablespoon
   concentrated tomato purée
300ml/½ pint concentrated
   soya milk

GARNISH
fresh tarragon leaves

Make the sauce first. Heat the margarine and oil in a large frying pan, and cook the onion and garlic without browning, until soft; stir all the time. Mix in the tomatoes, bay leaf, herbs and saffron, and simmer for 10 minutes until well blended. Pour in the stock and wine, and boil vigorously until the liquid is reduced by about one-third. Pass the sauce through a fine sieve, then press out the juice, leaving the pulp behind.

Season the flour with salt and pepper. Heat the oil for shallow frying in a pan large enough to take the turkey steaks in one layer. Toss them in the seasoned flour, then fry carefully for 3 minutes on each side, adding a little more hot oil, if required. Remove from the pan, and keep warm.

Pour off any oil left in the pan, then pour in the sieved sauce, and stir well to deglaze the pan. Mix in the tomato purée, then add the soya milk, stirring well, and heat through.

Put the turkey steaks on a hot serving dish, and pour over the sauce, coating the meat well. Garnish with tarragon leaves, and serve with plain boiled rice.

Finallys

By the time you have battled through the problems of what to make as a main course and how to start the meal, you then find yourself wrestling with the problem of a pudding or dessert. Of course, this is more of a problem for the kosher cook after a meat meal. Why not try Chestnut Charlotte which uses vegetarian block margarine and concentrated soya milk to produce a lavish dessert decorated with parve whipped cream? Alternatively, in Essex Pond Pudding, we use solid vegetable oil to replace suet in a tangy dish where the citrus juices mingle with the 'buttery' sauce as you cut it open.

Light ideas for people who cannot face the thought of a heavy pudding include recipes for a parve crème caramel and fruit mousse using eggs and gelatine to replace the more traditional cream.

There are more substantial puddings too – Rice Pudding for example, or Plum Pudding with Brandy 'Butter' – another surprise in a kosher cookbook.

For warm weather, we have a selection of ice creams – easy to make if you have a little time to spare – or, for a special treat, try Baked Alaska, which contrasts a hot baked meringue with an ice cream filling.

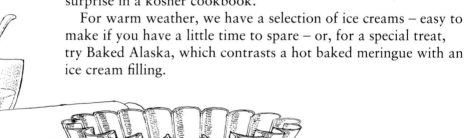

Plum Pudding

Mixed dried fruit is traditionally used today to replace the plums originally used for this festive pudding. It is well worth making in large quantities, and has a shelf-life of up to 12 months if well cooked and stored in a cool, dry dark cupboard. It should be made well in advance so that it can mature before eating.

Any leftover quantities can be sliced and fried in melted margarine.

100g/4 oz plain flour
1 × 2.5ml spoon/½ teaspoon
    ground ginger
1 × 2.5ml spoon/½ teaspoon
    mixed spice
1 × 2.5ml spoon/½ teaspoon
    ground nutmeg
a pinch of salt
450g/1 lb mixed dried fruit
50g/2 oz chopped almonds
225g/8 oz soft brown sugar
100g/4 oz fresh breadcrumbs
2 eggs, beaten
juice and grated rind of 1
    orange
300ml/½ pint dark beer **or**
    fruit juice with a few drops
    of liquid caramel
2 × 15ml spoons/2 tablespoons
    brandy (see **Note**)
150g/5 oz vegetarian block
    margarine, melted
margarine for greasing

Sift together the flour, ginger, mixed spice, nutmeg and salt into a bowl. Stir in the mixed dried fruit, chopped almonds, sugar and breadcrumbs.

In a separate bowl, beat together the eggs, orange juice and rind, most of the beer or fruit juice, the brandy and margarine. Stir this into the dry ingredients, mix together well, adding the remaining beer or fruit juice if necessary, to make a soft dropping consistency. Leave to stand for 2–3 hours to allow the flavours to blend; stir occasionally.

Divide the mixture between three greased and base-lined 600ml/1 pint basins. Cover with greaseproof paper and foil to seal them securely. Steam gently in a large saucepan for 4½–5 hours each, topping up the saucepan with boiling water as required. Leave for 5–10 minutes at room temperature to firm up, then store in a cool place until required.

Re-heat by steaming again for 1–1½ hours before serving.

Ignite with warmed brandy, and serve with Brandy 'Butter' or Parve Custard (page 61)

Note To enable the pudding to be removed from the saucepan without difficulty, it is a good idea to fold additional foil into long thin strips and to place them around the base and sides of each basin (before cooking) so that the edges can be used to remove each pudding.

Brandy 'Butter'

MAKES 100g/4 oz (approx)

100g/4 oz vegetarian block
    margarine
2 × 15ml spoons/2 tablespoons
    caster sugar
4 × 15ml spoons/4 tablespoons
    brandy

Cream together the margarine and sugar, then add the brandy, a few drops at a time. Put into a small serving dish, and chill until required.

Serve with Plum Pudding.

Parve Custard

a few drops vanilla essence
300ml/½ pint soya milk
2 eggs
50g/2 oz caster sugar

Mix together the vanilla essence and soya milk, then heat until almost boiling.

Whisk together the eggs and sugar, then add the hot soya milk, and whisk again until the sugar has dissolved. Return the mixture to the pan, and cook very gently, stirring all the time with a wooden spoon, until the mixture coats the back of the spoon. Serve hot.

Note For a thinner custard, use more soya milk.

Essex Pond Pudding

This is an adaptation of Sussex Pond Pudding which traditionally mixes suet and butter.

If you want to halve the quantities and make it for two people, use a lime instead of a lemon.

225g/8 oz plain flour, sifted
100g/4 oz solid vegetable oil
flour for rolling
margarine for greasing
100g/4 oz vegetarian block margarine, chopped
100g/4 oz Demerara sugar
1 lemon, washed and pierced with a skewer 8–10 times

Put the flour into a bowl, and rub in the solid vegetable oil as smoothly as possible – the slightly coarse texture does not affect the final appearance Bind with a little cold water, then roll out fairly thinly on a lightly floured surface.

Line a greased 900ml/1½ pint basin with three-quarters of the pastry. Put in half the margarine and half the sugar, then put the lemon in followed by the remaining margarine and sugar. Roll out the remaining pastry to fit the top of the basin. Dampen the rim, and place on top of the filling. Seal well. Cover the basin with greased foil, and tie securely with string.

Steam gently in a large saucepan for 3–3½ hours, topping up the saucepan with boiling water as required. Leave for 5–10 minutes at room temperature to firm up, then remove the foil.

To serve, invert the pudding onto a serving plate, and cut into wedges, ensuring that everyone has a piece of the lemon.

Rice Pudding

A non-dairy creamy rice pudding to follow a light meal.
Specially good on cold winter days.

50g/2 oz Carolina rice
600ml/1 pint soya milk
margarine for greasing
25g/1 oz sugar
grated nutmeg
15g/½ oz vegetarian block
   margarine

Soften the rice in the milk for 30 minutes in a greased 1.2 litre/2
pint ovenproof dish. Add the sugar, grate a little nutmeg over the
top, and dot with the margarine. Bake in a cool oven,
150°C/300°F/Gas 2, for about 2 hours until the rice is cooked and
the top is brown. Serve hot, with jam.

Indian Rice Pudding

100g/4 oz Carolina rice
600ml/1 pint soya milk
3 cardamom pods
50g/2 oz caster sugar
25g/1 oz chopped walnuts or
   almonds
grated nutmeg
silver leaf

Bring the rice to the boil in a little water, then boil for 2 minutes,
rinse and drain well.
   Bring the milk to the boil in a pan with the cardamom pods, then
add the rice, and simmer very slowly for 30 minutes, stirring
occasionally. Stir in the caster sugar and nuts, and cook until the
mixture resembles porridge. Remove the pan from the heat, discard
the cardamom pods, and transfer to a serving dish. Sprinkle with
the grated nutmeg, and decorate with the silver leaf. Serve warm or
cold.

Using soya milk, both Chicken in Lemon Sauce (page 40) and
Indian Rice Pudding can be served at one meal without
compromising any of the basic laws

Angelica Rice

100g/4 oz long-grain rice
350ml/12 fl oz soya milk
a pinch of salt
1 × 5ml spoon/1 teaspoon
   vanilla essence
3 eggs, separated
50g/2 oz sugar
40g/1½ oz angelica, chopped
margarine for greasing
2 × 15ml spoons/2 tablespoons
   dried cake crumbs

Bring the rice to the boil in a little water, then boil for 2 minutes, rinse and drain well.

Bring half the soya milk to the boil in a pan, then add the salt and vanilla essence. Mix in the rice, then simmer in a covered pan until the milk is absorbed.

Bring the remaining milk to the boil, then add it to the rice, a little at a time, until all the milk has been used and the rice is soft and creamy.

Beat the egg yolks lightly, then stir them into the rice with the sugar and angelica. Leave to cool.

Sprinkle a well greased 1.2 litre/2 pint ovenproof dish with the cake crumbs.

Beat the egg whites until stiff, then gently fold them into the rice mixture, a little at a time. Pour into the prepared dish, and bake in a moderate oven, 180°C/350°F/Gas 4, for 40 minutes until the rice is cooked and the top is brown. Leave in the oven with the door ajar to allow it to set. Turn out on to a warm dish to serve.

Walnut Cream

100g/4 oz granulated sugar
75ml/3 fl oz water
2 eggs, separated
1 × 15ml spoon/1 tablespoon
   cornflour
225ml/8 fl oz soya milk
50g/2 oz walnuts, chopped

DECORATION
parve whipped cream
   (page 94)
walnut halves

Heat half the sugar and all the water in a small saucepan, stirring all the time, until the sugar is dissolved completely and the syrup is clear. Boil rapidly, without stirring, until it turns a golden-brown colour. Mix well to dissolve the caramel, then remove from the heat.

Mix the remaining sugar, the egg yolks and cornflour with the soya milk, and heat gently in a small saucepan until the mixture thickens. Remove from the heat, add the caramel and the chopped walnuts, then leave to cool.

Beat the egg whites until stiff, then fold them gently into the cooled mixture. Spoon into individual ramekins, and decorate each one with whipped cream and walnut halves. Serve chilled.

Chestnut Charlotte

675g/1½ lb canned, sweetened
   chestnut purée
75g/3 oz stem ginger, drained
   and chopped
1 × 15ml spoon/1 tablespoon
   brandy
50g/2 oz vegetarian block
   margarine, softened
150ml/¼ pint concentrated
   soya milk
28 sponge fingers (approx)
oil for greasing

DECORATION
parve whipped cream
   (page 94)
strips angelica

Beat together the chestnut purée, ginger, brandy, margarine and soya milk.

Split one-third of the sponge fingers lengthways to form long, thin triangles, and use to make a circle on the base of a lightly oiled 17.5cm/7 inch charlotte mould or round cake tin. Arrange them with the points to the centre, making sure that the sugar side faces downwards. Line the sides with the remaining sponge fingers, sugar side outwards, fitting them closely and trimming to fit if necessary. Carefully spoon the chestnut mixture into the centre to fill the tin, and chill overnight to set.

Turn out of the tin, and decorate with whipped cream and angelica.

Lemon Mousse

1 × 15ml spoon/1 tablespoon
   parve gelatine
2 × 15ml spoons/2 tablespoons
   water
3 eggs, separated
100g/4 oz caster sugar
grated rind and juice of 1
   lemon
250g/9 oz imitation cream

Dissolve the gelatine in a pan with the water.

Meanwhile, cream the egg yolks, sugar and lemon rind until very pale and creamy.

Mix the lemon juice and dissolved gelatine, then heat until the liquid is clear; do not let it reach boiling point. Slowly mix into the creamed yolks, beating all the time, until cool and thick.

Whip half the imitation cream until soft peaks form, then fold gently into the lemon mixture.

Whisk the egg whites until stiff, then fold them in carefully into the lemon mixture. Pour into a 15–17.5cm/6–7 inch soufflé dish, and chill until set. Whip the remaining cream until stiff, and pipe swirls on top before serving.

Variation
To make an orange mousse, substitute the grated rind and juice of 2 oranges for the lemon.

Orange Mousse

A light and tangy way to end a meal.

3 eggs, separated
75g/3 oz caster sugar
2 × 15ml spoons/2 tablespoons
  cornflour
grated rind and juice of 1
  orange
150ml/¼ pint water
1 × 5ml spoon/1 teaspoon
  lemon juice
25g/1 oz vegetarian block
  margarine, chopped

Put the yolks, sugar and cornflour into a saucepan, and stir over low heat until well mixed together. Slowly add the orange rind and juice, the water and lemon juice, stirring well all the time. Raise the heat and continue stirring, adding the margarine slowly. Stir until the mixture thickens, then remove from the heat, and leave to cool.

Whisk the egg whites until stiff, then fold them carefully into the cooled orange mixture. Pour into individual serving dishes, and chill for at least 1 hour before serving.

Variation
To make a lemon mousse, substitute the grated rind and juice of 2 lemons for the orange, and increase the quantities of sugar to 100g/4oz.

Pear Meringue Tart

A delicious parve dessert to serve after a meat meal.

350g/12 oz prepared rich
  shortcrust pastry (page 89)
flour for rolling out
4 pears, peeled, halved and
  cored
75g/3 oz vanilla sugar (see
  Note)
1 × 5ml spoon/1 teaspoon
  powdered coriander
rind of ½ lemon
1 recipe quantity crème
  patissière (page 94)
3 egg whites
150g/5 oz caster sugar

Roll out the pastry on a lightly floured surface to fit a 25cm/10 inch flan tin. Prick the base with a fork, and bake blind in a fairly hot oven, 200°C/400°F/Gas 6, for 10 minutes, then remove the lining and continue baking for a further 10 minutes until crisp. Leave until cool.

Meanwhile, poach the pear halves in a single layer with the sugar, coriander, lemon rind and enough water barely to cover the pears. Cook until tender, then leave to cool.

Spread the Crème Patissière over the base of the cooled flan case. Drain the pear halves, and arrange them on top

Whisk the egg whites until stiff, add half the sugar and continue whisking until the mixture forms stiff peaks. Gently fold in the rest of the sugar, using a metal spoon. Use to pipe over the flan, or spread gently on top, and lift into peaks with the tip of a flat-bladed knife. Bake in a hot oven, 220°C/425°F/Gas 7, for a few minutes until the meringue begins to brown all over. Serve cold.

Notes
1. To make vanilla sugar, place a 5cm/2 inch vanilla pod in a tightly covered container of granulated or caster sugar. Leave until the flavours have infused.
2. The pastry case, cream mixture and fruit can be prepared well in advance. Assemble just before baking to prevent the pastry going soggy.

Pear Meringue Tart

Crème Caramel

4 × 15ml spoons/4 tablespoons
   granulated sugar
5 × 15ml spoons/5 tablespoons
   water
4 eggs
600ml/1 pint soya milk
1 × 2.5ml spoon/½ teaspoon
   vanilla essence
grated nutmeg

Heat 3 × 15ml spoons/3 tablespoons each of the sugar and water in a small saucepan, stirring all the time until the sugar is dissolved completely and the syrup is clear. Boil rapidly, without stirring, until it turns a golden-brown colour, then add the remaining water. Mix well to dissolve the caramel, then use quickly to coat the base and sides of a 17.5–20cm/7–8 inch ovenproof oval dish. Leave to cool.

Meanwhile, beat together the eggs and the remaining sugar. Gently warm the soya milk and the vanilla essence, then add to the egg mixture, stirring all the time. Strain the custard into the caramel-lined dish, and grate a little nutmeg over the top.

Stand the dish in a large baking tin containing 2.5cm/1 inch cold water. Bake in a cool oven, 150°C/300°F/Gas 2, for 1–1½ hours until the custard is set and firm. Chill well, then turn out carefully, and serve.

Variations
1. To make a coffee and rum flavoured Crème Caramel, beat in 2 × 15ml spoons /2 tablespoons rum with the eggs and sugar. Substitute 2 × 15ml spoons/2 tablespoons instant coffee powder for the vanilla essence. Omit the nutmeg.
2. Individual portions can be made by using small ramekins. Cook for 30–40 minutes only.

Iced Rum Mousse

4 eggs, separated
150g/5 oz caster sugar
4 × 15ml spoons/4 tablespoons
   white **or** dark rum
1 recipe quantity parve
   whipped cream (page 94)

Put the egg yolks into the top of a double boiler or into a bowl over a saucepan of boiling water. Add the sugar and rum, and heat very gently, stirring all the time with a wooden spoon until the mixture is thick. Do not overheat. Remove from the heat, and continue stirring until cold. Fold the whipped cream into the yolk mixture.

Whisk the egg whites until stiff, then gradually fold into the mixture, one-quarter at a time. Pour into a shallow container, and freeze until set.

Baked Alaska

1 × 20–22.5cm/8–9 inch
  sponge cake **or** sponge flan
  case
1 × 15ml spoon/1 tablespoon
  brandy (optional)
1 recipe quantity vanilla ice
  cream (page 70)
3 egg whites
a pinch of cream of tartar
75g/3 oz caster sugar

Place the sponge on a bread board or thick chopping board, and sprinkle with the brandy, if used. Shape the ice cream into a dome over the sponge, leaving a small border of about 1.25cm/½ inch on the outside of the cake. Return to the freezer.

Whisk the egg whites and cream of tartar until stiff, then gradually whisk in the sugar until the mixture forms stiff peaks. Spoon the meringue mixture carefully over the ice cream, working quickly but making sure that the ice cream is completely covered. Form the meringue into peaks with a palette knife. Bake in a very hot oven, 240°C/475°F/Gas 9, for 3–4 minutes until the meringue is lightly coloured. Serve at once.

Note Using a bread board or thick chopping board stops the heat being conducted upwards into the ice cream.

Variation
Put chopped fruit such as raspberries or peaches between the sponge and the ice cream.

Marmalade Ice Cream

300ml/½ pint soya milk
75g/3 oz caster sugar
3 eggs
4 × 15ml spoons/4 tablespoons
  orange marmalade

Heat the soya milk in a pan until almost scalding.

Beat together the sugar and eggs until thick, then whisk in the soya milk.

Return the mixture to the pan, and cook very gently, stirring all the time with a wooden spoon, until the mixture coats the back of the spoon. Do not overheat.

Strain through a sieve into a bowl over a bed of ice, and cool quickly. Stir in the marmalade.

Pour into a shallow container, and freeze for about 1½ hours until the middle begins to crystallize.

Remove from the freezer, then beat thoroughly to break up the ice crystals. Return to the freezer, and re-freeze until solid.

Remove from the freezer 20 minutes before serving.

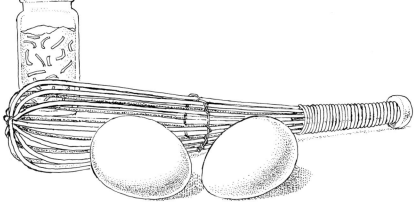

Vanilla Ice Cream

A good basic recipe using fresh soya milk to make the custard base.

600ml/1 pint soya milk
a few drops vanilla essence
150g/5 oz caster sugar
5 eggs, separated

Heat the soya milk in a pan until almost scalding, then add the vanilla essence.

Beat together the sugar and egg yolks until thick, then whisk in the soya milk.

Transfer the mixture to a clean pan, and cook gently, stirring all the time with a wooden spoon, until the mixture coats the back of the spoon. Do not overheat.

Strain through a sieve into a bowl over a bed of ice, and cool quickly.

Pour into a shallow container, and freeze for about 1½ hours until the middle begins to crystallize.

Remove from the freezer, then beat thoroughly to break up the ice crystals. Whisk the egg whites until stiff, then gradually fold into the half-frozen ice cream. Return to the freezer, and re-freeze until solid.

Remove from the freezer 20 minutes before serving.

Variations

CHOCOLATE ICE CREAM
Blend 40g/1½ oz sifted cocoa powder into the heated soya milk, then continue as above.

RUM AND RAISIN ICE CREAM
Soak 25g/1 oz raisins in 3 × 15ml spoons/3 tablespoons dark rum, and continue as above, adding the soaked raisins after the egg whites have been folded in. Use only 100g/4 oz sugar and omit the vanilla essence.

A selection of creamy parve ices
Vanilla, Chocolate **and** Marmalade (page 69) Ice Creams

Food for Passover

Passover can be a very difficult time of year for the Jewish cook – hands up if you think that it means eight days of matzos, cheese, potatoes, eggs and ground almonds! Here we set out to change all that – watch your guests' faces when you serve them Scotch Eggs or Chocolate Éclairs. What about Chicken and Courgette Lasagne or Parmigiana Bake? Have you ever been able to make quiches and flans for the Passover or Crêpes Suzette?

If you have ever been frustrated by the problems of catering at Passover, you will greet this chapter with delight. We have a host of recipes that maintain our international flavour even at this taxing time of year. We admit that you will have to use the odd matzo and egg in some, but the end results will revolutionize your Passover cookery.

Parsnip and Apple Soup

A creamy soup using eggs.

50g/2 oz vegetarian block margarine
675/1½ lb parsnips, roughly chopped
225g/8 oz cooking apples, peeled, cored and chopped
1.2 litres/2 pints well-flavoured stock
1 × 5ml spoon/1 teaspoon freshly chopped sage
1 × 5ml spoon/1 teaspoon freshly chopped parsley
salt, freshly ground black pepper
2 egg yolks, beaten

Melt the margarine in a medium-sized saucepan, and cook the parsnips and apples, tossing them well until coated with the fat. Cover the pan, and cook gently over low heat for 10–15 minutes, stirring occasionally, until the apple juices start to run. Pour in the stock, and add the sage, parsley and seasoning. Bring to the boil, then simmer gently for 30–40 minutes until the parsnips are soft.

Pass the soup through a sieve or purée in a blender or food processor. Return to the pan, and re-heat gently. Add a little soup to the beaten egg yolks, stirring well, then add the egg mixture to the soup, and re-heat gently, without allowing the soup to boil.

Serve with matzos and butter as a light meal.

Poûlet Normande

50g/2 oz vegetarian block margarine

1 × 15ml spoon/1 tablespoon vegetable oil

225g/8 oz Spanish onion, finely chopped

1 clove of garlic, crushed

fine matzo meal for coating

salt, freshly ground black pepper

1.35kg/3 lb roasting chicken, jointed

225g/8 oz apples, peeled, cored and diced

4 × 15ml spoons/4 tablespoons Passover brandy

1 × 15ml spoon/1 tablespoon finely chopped celery leaves

300ml/½ pint apple juice (see **Note**)

2 egg yolks, lightly beaten

GARNISH

sprigs watercress

apple slices, dipped in lemon juice to prevent discoloration

Heat the margarine and oil in a large frying pan, and cook the onion and garlic until transparent, stirring all the time.

Mix the matzo meal and seasoning, and use to coat the chicken portions lightly. Add to the pan in one layer, and cook until browned on both sides. Remove from the pan, and keep hot in an ovenproof dish.

Gently stir the apples into the pan, and cook for 2–3 minutes until softened. Pour in the brandy, and ignite it carefully. When the flames have died down, sprinkle in the celery leaves, pour over the apple juice, and bring to the boil.

Pour the contents of the pan over the chicken, cover tightly, and cook in a warm oven, 160°C/325°F/Gas 3, for 50–60 minutes until the chicken is tender and cooked through. Transfer the chicken to a large, warmed serving dish.

Pass the apple and the cooking juices through a sieve or purée in a blender or food processor. Bring to the boil, then boil rapidly until reduced to about 300ml/½ pint liquid. Add slowly to the beaten egg yolks, beating all the time to prevent the eggs curdling. Stir over very low heat until the mixture thickens, then pour it over the chicken. Garnish with sprigs of watercress and apple slices.

Note If Passover apple juice is not available, grate one large apple and squeeze firmly to extract the juice. Make up to 300ml/½ pint with water.

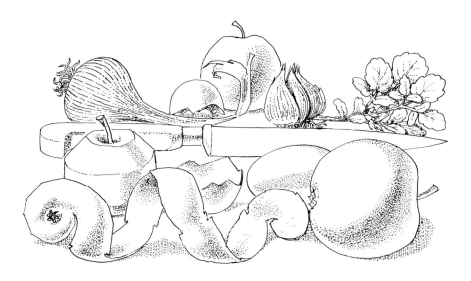

Chicken and Courgette Lasagne

2 × 15ml spoons/2 tablespoons
vegetable oil
1 medium onion, finely
chopped
350–400g/12–14 oz uncooked,
diced chicken breast meat
450g/1 lb courgettes, cut into
1.25cm/½ inch slices
1 × 5ml spoon/1 teaspoon
mixed herbs
1 × 5ml spoon/1 teaspoon
lemon juice
salt, freshly ground black
pepper
4–5 large matzos
white wine or chicken stock
1 recipe quantity Passover
white sauce (page 84)

Heat half the oil in a large frying pan, and cook the onion for 2 minutes until slightly softened. Add the chicken, and continue cooking, stirring well, until it is cooked through. Remove the onion and chicken from the pan, and keep warm.

Add the remaining oil to the pan, and fry the courgettes until lightly browned on each side. Remove from the pan and drain, if necessary. Add to the cooked chicken and onion, then add the herbs, lemon juice and seasoning.

Trim the matzos to fit a greased 17.5 × 25/7 × 10 inch ovenproof dish. Dip them in the wine or stock to soften them, then use some to line the dish. Put half the chicken and courgette mixture into the dish, then cover with another layer of matzo. Pour over half the white sauce, then repeat the layers, ending with the sauce. Bake in a fairly hot oven, 190°C/375°F/Gas 5, for 40 minutes until bubbling. Leave to rest for 5 minutes before serving.

Serve with a side salad.

Variation
Leftover cooked chicken can also be used. Fry the courgettes with the softened onions, remove from the heat, then leave to cool before adding 225–275g/8–10 oz diced cooked chicken. Ensure that all the ingredients are cold before assembling as above.

'Pasta' at Passover
Chicken and Courgette Lasagne

Chicken Kiev`

Chicken Kiev? And at Passover? Indeed yes, using margarine and matzo meal to replace the traditional butter and breadcrumbs.

grated rind and juice of 1
    lemon
25g/1 oz freshly chopped
    parsley
100g/4 oz vegetarian block
    margarine, softened
salt, freshly ground black
    pepper
a pinch of ground nutmeg
2 cloves garlic, crushed
6 chicken breasts, skinned and
    boned (see **Note**)
matzo meal for coating
beaten egg
oil for deep frying

Work the lemon rind and juice and the parsley into the margarine, and season to taste with the salt, pepper and nutmeg. Work in the garlic, then form into a roll, wrap in clingfilm, and chill for 2–3 hours.

Flatten each chicken breast with a rolling-pin, then cut the chilled garlic mixture into fingerlength pieces, and place 2–3 pieces in each chicken breast. Fold over and secure with cocktail sticks.

Coat each chicken portion first with matzo meal, then with beaten egg and finally with matzo meal again, pressing it in firmly. Chill for at least 1 hour to allow the coating to dry.

Heat the oil to 160°C/325°F, and deep fry the chicken for about 8 minutes or until the meat is cooked through and the coating is brown. Drain well on absorbent paper, and serve at once.

Notes
1. When boning the chicken, leave the top wing bone intact.
2. Do not allow the fat to be too hot when frying the chicken, as the outside will brown before the inside is cooked.

Scotch Eggs

350g/12 oz sausage-meat
a large pinch of grated
    nutmeg
2 × 15ml spoons/2 tablespoons
    mixed herbs
1 × 2.5ml spoon/½ teaspoon
    freshly chopped sage
salt, freshly ground black
    pepper
4 hard-boiled eggs
1 egg, beaten
medium matzo meal for
    coating
oil for deep frying

Mix the sausage-meat with the nutmeg, herbs, sage and seasoning, then divide into four equal portions.

With damp hands, work the sausage-meat round the eggs in an even layer. Roll the covered eggs first in the beaten egg, then toss gently in the matzo meal, pressing it in firmly. Chill for at least 15 minutes before frying so that the mixture firms up.

Heat the oil to 160°C/325°F, and deep fry the eggs, two at a time, until golden-brown all over. This should take about 5–6 minutes. Drain on absorbent paper.

Cut the eggs in half widthways, and serve hot, with grilled mushrooms and tomatoes, or cold, with a salad.

Corsican Paupiettes

175g/6 oz sausage-meat
1 large onion, very finely
  chopped
2 × 15ml spoons/2 tablespoons
  freshly chopped parsley
½ × 2.5ml spoon/¼ teaspoon
  allspice
½ × 2.5ml spoon/¼ teaspoon
  ground cinnamon
½ × 2.5ml spoon/¼ teaspoon
  ground nutmeg
salt, freshly ground black
  pepper
1–2 × 15ml spoons/1–2
  tablespoons medium matzo
  meal
4 ball of the rib steaks,
  100g/4 oz each (approx)
2 × 15ml spoons/2 tablespoons
  vegetable oil
1 large carrot, diced
1 clove of garlic, crushed
4 tomatoes, skinned, de-
  seeded and chopped
1 stalk of celery, diced
a pinch of fresh thyme
1 bay leaf
50ml/2 fl oz dry white wine
50g/2 oz green olives, stoned
1 egg yolk

Mix the sausage-meat with half the onion, the parsley, spices, salt and pepper, and add enough matzo meal to bind it together.

Flatten the steaks with a rolling-pin, and divide the stuffing mixture between the four pieces of meat, making sausage shapes at one end of the steaks. Roll the meat around the stuffing, making sure the mixture does not fall out. Tie each roll with fine string.

Heat the oil in a frying pan, and fry the rolls quickly to brown them all over. Remove from the pan, and keep warm.

Add the remaining onion, the carrot and garlic to the pan, and fry gently until golden-brown. Return the paupiettes to the pan, then add the tomatoes, celery, herbs, bay leaf, seasoning and wine. Cover the pan and simmer for 35 minutes. Add the olives, and continue cooking for about 10–15 minutes until the meat is tender. Remove the paupiettes from the pan, remove the string, and reserve the sauce. Transfer the meat to a warm serving dish.

Discard the bay leaf from the sauce, gently mix in the egg yolk mixed with a few drops of water, and immediately pour the sauce over the meat. Serve at once.

Mixed Vegetable Quiche

1 recipe quantity Passover
  pastry (2) (page 84)
2 × 15ml spoons/2 tablespoons
  vegetable oil
1 large onion, sliced
3 tomatoes, skinned, de-
  seeded and sliced
1 courgette, coarsely grated
1 large carrot, coarsely grated
2 stalks celery, finely sliced
3 eggs, beaten
150ml/¼ pint milk
salt, freshly ground black
  pepper
50g/2 oz hard cheese, grated

Roll out the pastry between two sheets of vegetable parchment to fit a 25cm/10 inch flan tin. Prick the base with a fork, and bake blind in a fairly hot oven, 200°C/400°F/Gas 6, for 20 minutes until the pastry began to brown. Leave until cool.

Meanwhile, heat the oil in a saucepan, and cook the onion until soft and transparent, stirring all the time. Add the remaining vegetables, and continue to cook until soft. Leave to cool, then spread over the base of the prepared pastry case.

Mix together the eggs and milk, and season to taste. Spoon gently over the vegetables in the pastry case, sprinkle with the grated cheese, and bake in a moderate oven, 180°C/350°F/Gas 4, for 35–40 minutes until set and brown.

Serve with a salad.

Note When baking blind, use crumpled foil instead of beans.

Cheese and Onion Flan

1 recipe quantity Passover
  pastry (1) (page 84)
2 × 15ml spoons/2 tablespoons
  vegetable oil
2 medium onions, chopped
2 eggs, beaten
150ml/¼ pint milk
225g/8 oz hard cheese, grated
salt, freshly ground black
  pepper

Roll out the pastry between two sheets of vegetable parchment to fit a 20cm/8 inch flan tin. Chill, preferably in a freezer, for 15–30 minutes.

Meanwhile, heat the oil in a small pan, and cook the onions gently until soft and transparent, stirring all the time.

Mix together the eggs and milk, add the onions and grated cheese, and season to taste. Pour the mixture into the prepared flan tin, and bake in a fairly hot oven, 190°C/375°F/Gas 5, for 35–40 minutes until set and golden. Serve hot or cold.

Note Do not worry if the pastry cracks while lining the dish. Patch it up, and smooth it together, ensuring that there are no gaps.

Pastry recipes for Passover
Mixed Vegetable Quiche **and** Cheese and Onion Flan

Parmigiana Bake

5 large matzos
4 eggs, lightly beaten
salt
oil for greasing
75g/3 oz hard cheese, grated

SAUCE
1 × 15ml spoon/1 tablespoon
   vegetable oil
1 medium onion, chopped
1 clove of garlic, chopped
1 green pepper, de-seeded and
   chopped
450g/1 lb tomatoes, skinned,
   de-seeded and chopped
1 × 15ml spoon/1 tablespoon
   freshly chopped parsley
salt, freshly ground black
   pepper

Soak the matzos in water for 10 minutes, then drain well, and break into pieces.

To make the sauce, heat the oil in a pan, and cook the onion and garlic for 2–3 minutes until transparent, stirring all the time. Add the pepper, and cook for a further 2–3 minutes. Add the tomatoes and parsley, and cook over low heat for about 20 minutes or until the tomatoes are cooked. Season to taste.

Season the eggs with salt, then stir in the matzo pieces. Put half the mixture into a large, greased ovenproof dish. Sprinkle with half the grated cheese, then cover with the remaining matzos. Sprinkle with the remaining cheese, and pour the tomato sauce on top. Bake uncovered, in a warm oven, 160°C/325°F/Gas 3, for 25–30 minutes until hot and bubbling. Serve hot, with a green salad.

Croquettes Lyonnais

5 large waxy potatoes, peeled
   and grated
50g/2 oz smoked salmon
   trimmings, chopped
1 clove of garlic, crushed
1 egg, beaten
1 × 15ml spoon/1 tablespoon
   freshly chopped parsley
salt, freshly ground black
   pepper
oil for shallow frying

Drain the grated potatoes in a colander, and pat dry in a cloth. Mix in a bowl with the salmon trimmings, garlic and egg, then add the parsley, and season to taste.

With damp hands, form the mixture into small balls, and flatten them slightly. Shallow fry in hot oil until golden-brown, then drain well, and serve hot as a light supper dish.

Variation
Substitute 50g/2 oz finely chopped salami for the smoked salmon.

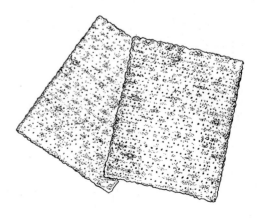

Crêpes Suzette

A Passover version of this classic dish.

100g/4 oz vegetarian block margarine, softened and diced
100g/4 oz caster sugar
75ml/3 fl oz orange-flavoured Passover liqueur
3 × 15ml spoons/3 tablespoons Passover brandy
finely grated rind and juice of 1 orange
1 recipe quantity Passover pancakes (2) (page 85)

Melt the margarine in a shallow frying pan. Remove the pan from the heat, then stir in the sugar, 2 × 15ml spoons/2 tablespoons of the orange liqueur and 1 × 15ml spoon/1 tablespoon of the brandy. Add the orange zest and juice. Return the pan to high heat, and boil rapidly for 1 minute to make a thick syrup, then reduce the heat so that the syrup simmers.

Add the pancakes, one at a time, folding them first in half and then into quarters. Lift them out of the pan, and keep warm on a heatproof plate over a pan of hot water.

Warm the remaining liqueur and brandy in a soup ladle, ignite and pour over the pancakes. Serve immediately the flames have died down.

Chocolate Farfel Roll

75ml/3 fl oz sweet dessert wine
2 × 5ml spoons/2 teaspoons Passover brandy
175g/6 oz matzo farfel **or** broken matzos
225g/8 oz vegetarian block margarine
225g/8 oz caster sugar
2 eggs
50g/2 oz cocoa powder
50g/2 oz chopped walnuts

Sprinkle the wine and brandy over the farfel or broken matzos, and leave for 10–15 minutes until softened.

Cream together the margarine and caster sugar, then beat in the eggs and cocoa powder. Add the softened farfel or matzos.

Spread the nuts evenly over a sheet of greaseproof paper, and spread the mixture evenly on top. Roll up like a Swiss roll so that the nuts are on the outside. Chill overnight. Serve thinly sliced.

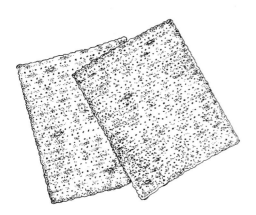

Lemony Almond Fingers

PASTRY
175g/6 oz potato flour
50g/2 oz matzo cake meal
25g/1 oz caster sugar
1 egg
150g/5 oz soft vegetarian
  margarine

FILLING
100g/4 oz ground almonds
100g/4 oz caster sugar
2 egg yolks
lemon curd

Put the pastry ingredients into a bowl, and mix together with a wooden spoon or process in a food processor. Wrap the pastry in greaseproof paper, and firm in the freezer for 10 minutes or in the refrigerator for 1 hour.

Meanwhile, mix together the ground almonds, caster sugar and egg yolks in a bowl.

Roll out the pastry between two sheets of vegetable parchment, and cut into two lengths, each $30 \times 6.25/12 \times 2\frac{1}{2}$ inches.

Dampen the pastry with a little water, and spread the filling carefully on top. Using a spoon handle, make a shallow depression along the centre of each bar. Return to the freezer for 10 minutes or the refrigerator for 1 hour to allow the pastry to rest.

Bake in a fairly hot oven, 190°C/375°F/Gas 5, for 15 minutes until the pastry is set and pale golden. Fill the channels with lemon curd, and bake for a further 10 minutes until the pastry is brown on top. Leave to cool, then cut each bar into fingers.

Chocolate Eclairs

MAKES 12–15

1 recipe quantity Passover
  choux pastry (page 86)
fat for greasing
150ml/¼ pint whipped cream

CHOCOLATE ICING
25g/1 oz parve plain
  chocolate, broken into
  squares
  2 × 15ml spoons/2
  tablespoons vegetable oil
75g/3 oz icing sugar, sifted
2 × 15ml spoons/2 tablespoons
  hot water

Spoon the pastry into a large nylon forcing bag fitted with a 2cm/¾ inch plain nozzle. Pipe éclairs 7.5cm/3 inches long on to a greased baking tray, leaving plenty of space between each one to allow for expansion. Use a knife to cut the end of each éclair smoothly whilst piping. Bake in a hot oven, 220°C/425°F/Gas 7, for 10 minutes, then reduce the heat to fairly hot, 190°C/375°F/Gas 5, and bake for a further 15–20 minutes until well risen and brown. Make a slit in one long side of each éclair to allow the steam to escape, then cool on a wire rack.

Meanwhile, make the chocolate icing. Melt the chocolate with the oil in a small bowl over gently steaming water. Mix the icing sugar with the hot water, then stir into the melted chocolate. Beat well until smooth and thick enough to coat the back of a spoon. Keep warm.

Pipe or spoon the whipped cream into the slits in the sides of the éclairs, then spread the tops of each one with the chocolate icing, and leave until set.

Tea-time at Passover
Chocolate Eclairs **and** Lemony Almond Fingers

Passover White Sauce

MAKES 450ml/¾ pint (approx)

3 × 15ml spoons/3 tablespoons
   vegetable oil
1 clove of garlic (optional)
25g/1 oz potato flour
450ml/¾ pint chicken stock
salt, white pepper
2 egg yolks, lightly beaten

Heat the oil in a small saucepan, then fry the garlic, if using. Remove from the pan. Mix the potato flour with the stock, and season to taste. Blend in the yolks, then add to the pan. Cook very gently over moderate heat until the sauce thickens, stirring all the time to prevent curdling.

Use as required.

Passover Pastry (1)

MAKES 150g/5 oz (approx)

75g/3 oz fine matzo meal
1 × 5ml spoon/1 teaspoon
   Passover baking powder
a pinch of salt
50g/2 oz vegetarian block
   margarine
1 egg, beaten

Mix together the matzo meal, baking powder and salt, then rub in the margarine until the mixture resembles fine breadcrumbs. Stir in the egg to form a ball of dough, adding a few drops of cold water if necessary.

Use as required.

Passover Pastry (2)

MAKES 350g/12 oz (approx)

This pastry is suitable for sweet or savoury flans.

175g/6 oz fine matzo meal
50g/2 oz potato flour
a pinch of salt **or** 1 × 5ml
   spoon/1 teaspoon caster
   sugar
2–3 × 15ml spoons/2–3
   tablespoons iced water
   (approx)
100g/4 oz vegetarian block
   margarine

Mix together the matzo meal, potato flour, salt or sugar, then rub in the margarine until the mixture resembles fine breadcrumbs. Sprinkle in the water, a little at a time, and press the dough together to form a ball. Wrap in clingfilm, then chill for at least 30 minutes to firm up.

Use as required.

Passover Pancakes (1)

A very fine, thin pancake suitable for rolling.

2 eggs
100ml/4 fl oz water
a pinch of salt
50g/2 oz potato flour
2 × 5ml spoons/2 teaspoons
    vegetable oil
oil for greasing

Beat together the eggs, water, salt, potato flour and oil until smooth, then leave to stand for 5 minutes.

Heat a 17.5cm/7 inch frying pan, and oil it very lightly. Remove from the heat, and pour in just enough batter to coat the base thinly, tilting the pan quickly so that the batter spreads evenly. Return the pan to the heat, and fry the pancake until the edges curl away from the sides and the underside is golden. Repeat with the other side.

Turn the cooked pancake on to a clean cloth so that it falls out with the cooked side on top. Cover and keep warm. Continue cooking the remaining batter until it has been used up.

Use as required.

Note Keep stirring the batter well to stop the potato flour separating.

Passover Pancakes (2)

A softer, slightly thicker pancake, more suited to layering and folding.

2 eggs, beaten
a pinch of salt
75g/3 oz matzo cake meal
300ml/½ pint water

Beat together the eggs, salt and cake meal, then add the water slowly, beating well to make a thin batter. Leave to stand for 30 minutes, then beat again to ensure it is smooth.

Heat a 17.5cm/7 inch frying pan, and oil it very lightly. Remove from the heat, and pour in just enough batter to coat the base thinly, tiliting the pan quickly so that the batter spreads evenly. Return the pan to the heat, and fry the pancake until the edges curl away from the sides and underside is golden. Repeat with the other side.

Turn the cooked pancake on to a clean cloth, and cover to keep warm. Continue cooking the remaining batter until it has been used up.

Use as required.

Passover Choux Pastry

Use the conventional choux pastry method but substitute a very finely ground matzo meal for flour.

150ml/¼ pint water
50g/2 oz vegetarian block margarine
75g/3 oz very fine matzo cake meal
a pinch of salt
2 small eggs

Heat together the water and margarine in a saucepan, stirring until the fat has melted. Bring to the boil, then remove from the heat.

Sift together the matzo meal and salt. Add to the liquid, then beat the mixture together. Return the pan to gentle heat, and continue to beat until the dough is smooth and leaves the sides of the pan clean. Remove from the heat, leave to cool slightly, then beat in the eggs, one at a time. Continue beating until the mixture is very smooth and shiny.

Use as required.

Variation
To double the quantity, use 3 large eggs.

Fundamentals

Here are some of the basic recipes and techniques essential for following our new style of kosher cookery – you will find references to this chapter throughout the book. However, this does not mean that you should not use some of these basic ideas to follow your own paths and create your own dishes – or perhaps convert some other recipes to kosher cookery, once you have seen how easy it is to do. Here you will see how soya milk, eggs and vegetarian margarine are used in place of animal fats and the traditional dairy products, opening up a whole new world to the kosher cook.

Tortillas, for example, can be served with a variety of fillings – what about putting some Chilli con Carne inside each one and serving it with some finely shredded lettuce on top? How about trying Parve Hollandaise Sauce with fresh asparagus before a meat main course or ending a meal with a flourish – with Crêpes Suzette, substituting the basic pancake recipe in this chapter for the Passover pancakes on page 85? We have included one traditional recipe in this chapter – Mandelen, the perfect accompaniment to our earlier cream soup recipes – because we cannot find a recipe anywhere to beat this one.

Vegetarian White Sauce

MAKES 300ml/½ pint (approx)

20g/¾ oz vegetarian block margarine
20g/¾ oz flour
300ml/½ pint soya milk
salt, white pepper

Melt the margarine in a pan, and stir in the flour. Cook over low heat for 2–3 minutes, stirring constantly with a wooden spoon. Gradually add the soya milk, beating vigorously so that the mixture comes away from the sides of the pan. Keep stirring while adding the soya milk, taking care that no lumps form. When all the soya milk has been added, bring the sauce to the boil, then simmer for 5 minutes, stirring all the time. Season to taste, and use as required.

Variation
For a thinner sauce, add more soya milk. For a thicker sauce, use 25g/1 oz each of margarine and flour.

Rich White Sauce

A very creamy white sauce.

40g/1½ oz vegetarian block
    margarine
25g/1 oz plain flour
salt, white pepper
225ml/8 fl oz chicken stock
50ml/2 fl oz white wine
a pinch of ground nutmeg
1 egg yolk

Melt 25g/1 oz margarine in a small saucepan. Stir in the flour and
seasoning, and cook over low heat for 1 minute without browning;
stir constantly with a wooden spoon.

Gradually add the stock and wine, stirring all the time, and cook,
stirring, until the sauce is thick and smooth. Add the nutmeg.

Cut the remaining margarine into small pieces, then add it slowly
to the pan with the egg yolk, beating all the time until the sauce
whitens. Alternatively, process in a blender or food processor, and
blend until white.

Use as required.

Parve Hollandaise Sauce

3 × 15ml spoons/3 tablespoons
    cider vinegar
3 × 15ml spoons/3 tablespoons
    water
50g/2 oz onions, finely
    chopped
8 black peppercorns
1 bay leaf
1 × 5ml spoon/1 teaspoon
    dried mixed herbs
3 egg yolks
150g/5 oz vegetarian block
    margarine, softened

Put the vinegar and water into a small saucepan, and add the
onions, peppercorns, bay leaf and herbs. Bring to the boil, then
simmer until the onion is soft. Raise the heat, and boil vigorously
until the liquid has reduced to about 1 tablespoon. Leave to cool,
then strain through a sieve.

Cream the egg yolks with a walnut-sized piece of the margarine
until well blended. Add the strained vinegar, and stir well. Place the
bowl over a pan of boiling water, then carefully whisk in the
remaining margarine, a little at a time, until the sauce is shiny and
resembles mayonnaise. (If the sauce starts to separate, quickly dip
the bowl in a dish of cold water to reduce the heat, then beat
vigorously.) Alternatively, process in a blender or food processor
but strain the vinegar while hot, and melt the margarine until
bubbling before pouring it into the goblet with the other
ingredients. Use warm, as required.

Shortcrust Pastry

225g/8 oz plain flour
1 × 2.5ml spoon/½ teaspoon salt
100g/4 oz vegetarian block margarine, cut into small pieces
2–3 × 15ml spoons/2–3 tablespoons cold water
flour for rolling out

Sift the flour and salt into a mixing bowl, then rub in the margarine with the tips of the fingers until the mixture resembles fine breadcrumbs. Sprinkle the water on to the surface, and mix it with a round-bladed knife until it forms large lumps. Push the dough together with the tips of the fingers, and sweep it round the edge to make sure that all the crumbs are collected.

Turn out on to a floured surface, and knead lightly until firm. Leave to rest for at least 30 minutes in a cool place before using it.

Use as required.

Rich Shortcrust Pastry

This pastry, similar to the French pâte sucrée, is ideal for sweet flans, tartlets or fruit pies.

250g/9 oz plain flour
a pinch of salt
150g/5 oz vegetarian block margarine, cut into small pieces
1 egg, beaten
50g/2 oz caster sugar
flour for rolling out

Sift the flour and salt into a mixing bowl, then rub in the margarine with the tips of the fingers until the mixture resembles breadcrumbs. Make a well in the centre, add the egg and sugar, and mix with a round-bladed knife until a smooth dough is obtained. Add a very little water, if necessary, if the mixture seems too dry.

Turn out on to a floured surface, and knead lightly until smooth. Leave to rest for at least 30 minutes in a cool place before using it.

Use as required.

Puff Pastry

MAKES 450g/1 lb (approx)

Traditionally made with lard, this kosher version, made with vegetarian margarine, is suited both to milk and meat recipes.

225g/8 oz plain flour
1 × 5ml spoon/1 teaspoon salt
225g/8 oz vegetarian block margarine, cut into small pieces
150ml/¼ pint iced water
1 × 5ml spoon/1 teaspoon lemon juice
flour for rolling out

Sift the flour and salt into a mixing bowl. Add one-quarter of the margarine, and rub it into the flour, using the fingertips. Add the water and lemon juice, and mix the ingredients into a firm ball with a round-bladed knife.

Turn out on to a lightly floured surface, and knead until smooth. On a lightly floured surface, roll it into a rectangle approximately 15 × 20cm/6 × 8 inches. Cut the remaining margarine into small pieces, and spread over the top two-thirds of the rectangle. Fold the uncovered third up and the top third down, and turn the pastry 90° so that the folds are at the top and bottom. Roll out the pastry again to a similar size, then re-fold it, wrap in clingfilm, and chill for at least 1 hour.

Repeat the rolling and folding four more times, letting the pastry rest for a further hour after the second two times, and a further hour before using it.

Use as required.

Vegetarian Pancakes

100g/4 oz plain flour
a pinch of salt
1 egg
1 egg yolk
450ml/¾ pint soya milk
oil for shallow frying

Sift the flour and salt into a bowl. Make a well in the centre, then add the egg, egg yolk and soya milk. Beat well to form a smooth batter, using an electric hand-held mixer if available. Leave the batter to stand for at least 30 minutes, then beat well again to ensure that no lumps of flour remain.

Heat a 15–17.5cm/6–7 inch frying pan, and oil it very lightly. Remove from the heat, and pour in just enough batter to coat the base thinly, tilting the pan quickly so that the batter spreads evenly. Return to the heat, and fry the pancake until lightly browned. Repeat with the other side. Continue to cook all the pancakes, stacking the completed ones on a plate until required. Add a little more oil to the pan during cooking, if necessary.

Use as required.

Note The pancakes can be made in advance and frozen for 2 months.

Soya milk is the ingredient common to both the pancakes and filling for Chicken and Mushroom Pancakes (page 56)

Tortillas

Masa harina is fine cornmeal and can be brought in specialist shops or good delicatessens.

250g/9 oz masa harina
1 × 2.5ml spoon/½ teaspoon
  salt
225ml/8 fl oz warm water

Mix the masa harina and salt in a bowl, then slowly add the water, mixing with a fork, until it forms together. Add more water if necessary, but ensure that the mixture is not too wet – it should just hold together.

Knead the dough lightly with one hand until smooth and free from cracks. Divide into 12 equal pieces, and shape each piece into a ball. Keep covered, while rolling out each tortilla, to stop them drying out.

Flatten one ball slightly, then roll it out between two sheets of waxed paper until it is a 15cm/6 inch round. Remove the bottom sheet of paper.

Heat a frying pan, and put the tortilla into the pan. Remove the top sheet, and cook for 30 seconds until the edges turn up. Turn it over and cook the other side, pressing down gently with a spatula. Turn it again, and cook for a further minute until the underside is lightly brown and speckled. Repeat with the remaining mixture, then stack the cooked tortillas together, and wrap in foil.

Use as required.

Garlic Croûtons

3 slices French bread, crusts
  removed
oil for frying
2 cloves garlic, halved

Cut the bread into 1.25cm/½ inch cubes. Heat the oil in a frying pan, and add the garlic cloves, then remove them. Fry the bread cubes until golden-brown, then drain well on absorbent paper.

Use as required.

Aunt Celia's Mandelen

This traditional recipe was given to us by a favourite aunt, who made them for her family until well into her 100th year, and we have never tasted any to beat them.

2 × 15ml spoons/2 tablespoons cooking oil
2 × 5ml spoons/2 teaspoons salt
3 eggs, beaten
275g/10 oz plain flour, sifted flour
oil for deep frying

Mix together the oil, salt and beaten eggs.

Sift the flour on to a pastry board, make a well in the centre, and pour in the egg mixture. Gradually mix in the flour to make a soft dough. If it feels too stiff, add a little extra oil; knead well until smooth.

Keeping the bulk of the dough covered with a damp cloth, break off a piece about the size of a small egg, and roll it between well-floured hands into a long thin roll about 0.5cm/$\frac{1}{4}$ inch thick. Leave to dry on the pastry board for about 10 minutes while rolling out the remaining dough.

Sprinkle the surface with flour, then, using scissors, snip the rolls into 0.5cm/$\frac{1}{4}$ inch triangles. Leave to dry for a further 30 minutes.

Heat the oil to 180°C/350°F, shake off the surplus flour, and deep fry the mandelen, a few at a time, until light golden. Remove from the oil with a perforated spoon, then drain in a colander.

Use as required.

Note These are a good stand-by and can be stored for several weeks in a screw-topped jar or frozen for 3 months.

Parve Cream

MAKES 300ml/$\frac{1}{2}$ pint (approx)

300ml/$\frac{1}{2}$ pint soya milk
2 × 15ml spoons/2 tablespoons cornflour
50g/2 oz soft vegetarian margarine
25g/1 oz caster sugar

Mix 2 × 15ml spoons/2 tablespoons of the soya milk with the cornflour until smooth. Heat the remaining soya milk in a small saucepan, and pour it quickly on to the cornflour mixture, stirring vigorously. Return to the heat, and cook gently until the mixture thickens, stirring all the time. Leave to cool.

Cream the margarine and sugar until soft and creamy, then beat it into the cornflour mixture, a spoonful at a time.

Use as required.

Parve Whipped Cream

MAKES 300ml/½ pint (approx)

2 × 5ml spoons/2 teaspoons
  parve gelatine
300ml/½ pint water
50g/2 oz soft vegetarian
  margarine
100g/4 oz powdered soya milk
sugar

Dissolve the gelatine in a pan with 2 × 15ml spoons/2 tablespoons of the water. Heat until the liquid is clear; do not let it reach boiling point. Add the margarine, the powdered soya milk and the remaining water, then beat well until thoroughly blended. Sweeten to taste. Chill for 2–3 hours, then beat until well whipped. Alternatively, process in a blender or food processor for 1 minute, then chill. Blend again before using.

Use as required.

Crème Patissière

MAKES 600ml/1 pint (approx)

A parve version of the traditional French pastry filling.

450ml/¾ pint soya milk
3 egg yolks
75g/3 oz granulated sugar
40g/1½ oz plain flour
1 × 5ml spoon/1 teaspoon
  vanilla essence

Heat the soya milk gently in a small saucepan.

Cream together the yolks, sugar and flour. Whisk in the hot soya milk, then return it to the pan and bring back to the boil, stirring all the time. Simmer for a further 2 minutes to cook the flour, then leave to cool.

Use as required.

St Honoré Pastry Cream

MAKES 750ml/1¼ pints (approx)

A fluffier and lighter version of Crème Patissière. Suitable for gâteaux.

3 egg whites
a pinch of salt
1 recipe quantity prepared
  crème patissière
2 × 15ml spoons/2 tablespoons
  orange liqueur

Whisk the egg whites with a pinch of salt until very stiff.

Bring the Crème Patissière carefully to boiling point, then stir in the liqueur. Remove from the heat, and leave to cool slightly before folding in 2 × 15ml spoons/2 tablespoons of the whisked egg whites. Gradually fold in the remaining whites until the cream is light and fluffy.

Use as required.

Mincemeat

Margarine replaces the suet, traditionally used in this recipe.

450g/1 lb cooking apples,
  coarsely grated
450g/1 lb mixed dried fruit,
  chopped
50g/2 oz currants
50g/2 oz raisins, halved
50g/2 oz mixed dried peel
225g/8 oz Demerara sugar
25g/1 oz chopped almonds
rind and juice of 1 lemon
1 × 2.5ml spoon/½ teaspoon
  ground nutmeg
a pinch of ground cloves
a pinch of ground cinnamon
½ × 2.5ml spoon/¼ teaspoon
  salt
225g/8 oz vegetarian block
  margarine, melted
3 × 15ml spoons/3 tablespoons
  brandy

Mix together the apples, all the dried fruits, the sugar, almonds, lemon rind and juice, the spices and salt. Stir in the margarine, and add the brandy. Leave overnight so that the fruit can absorb the liquid.

Pack into sterilized jars, leaving 2.5cm/1 inch headspace to allow for expansion. Cover tightly with clingfilm, and leave for at least 1 week for the flavours to blend and mature. Store in a cool, dry place.

Use with shortcrust (page 89) or puff (page 90) pastry to make pies, or serve warmed as a topping for ice cream (see pages 69–70).

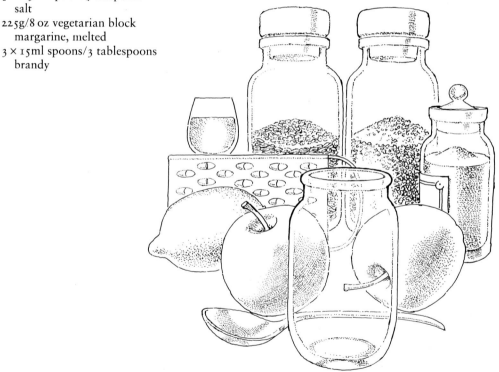

Index